Political Culture, Soft Interventions and Nation Building

This book raises questions about cultural interventions, an area of investigation somewhat overlooked in place of developing a critique of political interventions. Whilst political interventions are more explicit, coercive, and have a wide-reaching impact, it is important also to examine the way culture is used in attempts to reconstruct society and peoples —the 'soft' side of statebuilding, where heritage is utilized to play a role in the construction of the nation and the people, in memory and identity. For it can play a role in legitimizing myths and identifying symbolic, historic events, and implicitly informs the construction of infrastructure, institutions, and other aspects of civic life. Contributors from the fields of politics, anthropology, archaeology, and sociology examine interventions in state and nation building through cultural methods, the 'soft' side of statebuilding, including the preservation and promotion of certain heritage, the politics of remembrance and monument building, and the repatriation of human remains and artefacts to communities in the name of making reparations for past atrocities.

These are timely contributions. Heritage and cultural is too often considered in terms of how tourism might contribute to the economy post-conflict, neglecting the construction of meaning and memory through decisions about what is preserved or not. This book will be of special interest to those in the field of cultural studies, archaeology, and politics as well as international relations.

This book was originally published as a special issue of the *Journal of Intervention and Statebuilding*.

Tiffany Jenkins is a Sociologist and cultural commentator. Her research examines conflicts over cultural property and concepts of cultural value. She is the co-editor of the culture section of *Sociology Compass*, a regular broadcaster and contributor to the national press. http://tiffanyjenkinsinfo.wordpress.com/.

Political Culture, Soft Interventions and Nation Building

Edited by
Tiffany Jenkins

LONDON AND NEW YORK

First published 2015
by Routledge
2 Park Square, Milton Park, Abingdon, Oxon, OX14 4RN, UK

and by Routledge
711 Third Avenue, New York, NY 10017, USA

Routledge is an imprint of the Taylor & Francis Group, an informa business

© 2015 Taylor & Francis

All rights reserved. No part of this book may be reprinted or reproduced or utilised in any form or by any electronic, mechanical, or other means, now known or hereafter invented, including photocopying and recording, or in any information storage or retrieval system, without permission in writing from the publishers.

Trademark notice: Product or corporate names may be trademarks or registered trademarks, and are used only for identification and explanation without intent to infringe.

British Library Cataloguing in Publication Data
A catalogue record for this book is available from the British Library

ISBN 13: 978-1-138-79356-9

Typeset in Helvetica
by Taylor & Francis Books

Publisher's Note
The publisher accepts responsibility for any inconsistencies that may have arisen during the conversion of this book from journal articles to book chapters, namely the possible inclusion of journal terminology.

Disclaimer
Every effort has been made to contact copyright holders for their permission to reprint material in this book. The publishers would be grateful to hear from any copyright holder who is not here acknowledged and will undertake to rectify any errors or omissions in future editions of this book.

Contents

Citation Information	vii
Notes on Contributors	ix

1. Introduction
   Tiffany Jenkins — 1

2. Reconstructing Heritage in the Aftermath of Civil War: Re-Visioning the Nation and the Implications of International Involvement
   Dacia Viejo-Rose — 7

3. International Constructions of National Memories: The Aims and Effects of Foreign Donors' Support for Genocide Remembrance in Rwanda
   Rachel Ibreck — 31

4. Claims to the Past. A Critical View of the Arguments Driving Repatriation of Cultural Heritage and Their Role in Contemporary Identity Politics
   Liv Nilsson Stutz — 52

5. A Many-Cornered Thing: The Role of Heritage in Indian Nation-Building
   Brian Hole — 78

Index — 105

Citation Information

The chapters in this book were originally published in the *Journal of Intervention and State-building,* volume 7, issue 2 (June 2013). When citing this material, please use the original page numbering for each article, as follows:

Chapter 1
Introduction to the Special Issue on Cultural Interventions
Tiffany Jenkins
Journal of Intervention and Statebuilding, volume 7, issue 2 (June 2013) pp. 119–124

Chapter 2
Reconstructing Heritage in the Aftermath of Civil War: Re-Visioning the Nation and the Implications of International Involvement
Dacia Viejo-Rose
Journal of Intervention and Statebuilding, volume 7, issue 2 (June 2013) pp. 125–148

Chapter 3
International Constructions of National Memories: The Aims and Effects of Foreign Donors' Support for Genocide Remembrance in Rwanda
Rachel Ibreck
Journal of Intervention and Statebuilding, volume 7, issue 2 (June 2013) pp. 149–169

Chapter 4
Claims to the Past. A Critical View of the Arguments Driving Repatriation of Cultural Heritage and Their Role in Contemporary Identity Politics
Liv Nilsson Stutz
Journal of Intervention and Statebuilding, volume 7, issue 2 (June 2013) pp. 170–195

Chapter 5
A Many-Cornered Thing: The Role of Heritage in Indian Nation-Building
Brian Hole
Journal of Intervention and Statebuilding, volume 7, issue 2 (June 2013) pp. 196–222

Please direct any queries you may have about the citations to
clsuk.permissions@cengage.com

Notes on Contributors

Brian Hole is a Doctoral Student at the UCL Institute of Archaeology, UK, focusing on issues of identity and community with regard to Indian heritage sites.

Rachel Ibreck is a Lecturer in Peace and Conflict Studies at the University of Limerick, Ireland. She completed a PhD in the Politics of Memory in Post-Genocide Rwanda at the University of Bristol, UK, in 2009.

Tiffany Jenkins is a Sociologist and cultural commentator. She is the co-editor of the culture section of *Sociology Compass* and the author of *Contesting Human Remains in Museum Collections: The Crisis of Cultural Authority* (2010). She writes regularly for the broadsheets on cultural issues, http://tiffanyjenkinsinfo.wordpress.com.

Liv Nilsson Stutz is an Archaeologist and Anthropologist who is interested in ritual and body theory and the methodological approaches to reconstructing mortuary practices in the past from archaeological sources. She also has a strong interest in the use of cultural heritage in contemporary identity production, and has conducted a comparative study on the repatriation debate in an international perspective. She works as a Lecturer in the Anthropology Department at Emory University, UK.

Dacia Viejo-Rose took up a three-year British Academy Post-Doctoral Fellowship in January 2012; her research topic is 'Cultural Violence/Violence against Culture'. Since 2006 she has been teaching and supervising undergraduate and graduate students on Heritage at the Department of Archaeology, University of Cambridge, UK. Her PhD (2009) from Cambridge focused on the reconstruction of cultural heritage after civil war and its long-term impacts on societies. She has recently published her first monograph *Reconstructing Spain: Cultural Heritage and Memory after Civil War* (2011).

Introduction

Tiffany Jenkins

This special issue aims to raise questions about cultural interventions, an area of investigation somewhat overlooked in place of developing a critique of political interventions. Whilst political interventions are more explicit, coercive and have a wide-reaching impact, it is important also to examine the way culture is used in attempts to reconstruct society and peoples—the 'soft' side of statebuilding, where heritage is utilized to play a role in the construction of the nation and the people, in memory and identity. For it can play a role in legitimizing myths and identifying symbolic, historic events, and implicitly informs the construction of infrastructure, institutions and other aspects of civic life.

In the aftermath of the destruction of historical and artistic monuments across Europe during World War II, the Hague Convention of 1954 recognized the significance of cultural property—monuments and buildings—and outlined that it should be protected and conserved in times of war, because it was civilian property. More recently, the definition of cultural heritage and what it is for has expanded. The idea of intangible heritage—that which is not physical buildings or monuments, but social practices, oral traditions, knowledge and skills—has become prominent. The United Nations Educational, Scientific and Cultural Organization (UNESCO) adopted the Convention for the Safeguarding of the Intangible Cultural Heritage in 2003, entering force in 2006, and it outlines that cultural expression requires protection. According to the 2003 Convention, the intangible cultural heritage is so defined and deemed essential for the following:

> Intangible Cultural Heritage means the practices, representations, expressions, knowledge, skills—as well as the instruments, objects, artifacts and cultural spaces associated therewith—that communities, groups and, in some cases, individuals recognize as part of their cultural heritage. This intangible cultural heritage, transmitted from generation to generation, is constantly recreated by communities and groups in response to their environment, their interaction with nature and their history, and provides them with a sense of identity and continuity, thus promoting respect for cultural diversity and human creativity.[1]

Cultural heritage has been attributed extra, almost causal, properties. Cultural heritage—physical and intangible—is seen as an essential component in affirming and preserving cultural identity. With an expansion in what cultural heritage is, together with an expansion in what it is considered to 'do', scrutiny is timely.

Contributors to this special issue thus examine interventions through cultural methods, focusing on cases that promote the preservation of particular heritage; monument building in post-conflict societies; and the repatriation of human remains and artefacts to communities in the name of making reparations for past atrocities. All address the assumptions and consequences behind such interventions.

Dacia Viejo-Rose analyses the reconstruction of heritage in the aftermath of civil war. Heritage, especially post-war, is often a site where nations and communities construct and contest a past and a future. As certain sites and buildings are selected for preservation, concrete form is given to a re-visioned nation, shifting the boundaries of who belongs and who does not. For Viejo-Rose, it is important to question the common attribution to heritage as intrinsically positive, because it can also be a locus of conflict. In the reconstruction processes communal antagonisms can be compounded rather than securing reconciliation. Her article examines the Spanish Civil War of 1936–39 and the Bosnian War of 1992–95 as case studies. Despite the differences in time and space, in both cases the protection and destruction of cultural heritage was used in propaganda battles and the international community became actively concerned with it. Her studies provide illustrations of the potentially antagonizing nature of heritage and public monuments. She looks at some of the potential tensions and difficulties with such outside interventions, especially when outsiders may have a different agenda, varied and different experience to the locals, and a more short-term focus. She highlights how concepts of a universal heritage are imposed but do not correspond with the vision of heritage on the ground and the problems therein.

Rachel Ibreck examines the construction of heritage in post-conflict state-building in Rwanda, looking at the genocide memorials, focusing on the Kigali Genocide Memorial Centre (KMC). She notes how memorialization can be a mechanism for asserting political interests at home, but concentrates on how, in recent times, it has also served to extend the remit of international actors. The KMC is an example of transnational memory making. Whilst it originated with national elites, the idea was inspired by international Holocaust memorials. Ibreck reveals tensions in the agenda, which seeks to construct both national identity and an imagined 'international community'. For Ibreck, this project illuminates international donors' ambitions and demonstrates the extent of their involvement in the re-imagining of Rwanda, reflecting a global trend towards 'post-national' commemoration. As with the domestic state, international agencies respond to challenges posed to their legitimacy by an event in which they were implicated. Like national elites, they produce an idea of the nation through commemoration, and they use memorials to assert their difference from those responsible for past atrocities and to construct moral legitimacy. National and international practices of memory have become fused as each seeks legitimacy from the other. She suggests that this national remembrance firms up domestic legitimacy, and secures ruling elites within international frameworks. This is a significant departure, Ibreck ventures, where the national hold on memory has been loosened by international norms, finance and narratives. Memorialization has always been an important area of attention; in order to understand the vision of the past that is used to forge the idea of the nation in the future. In recent times, however, as Ibreck highlights, international actors have become more involved, and extended their remit for their international and domestic interests. Further, it is an important area of analysis because of its expansion. In the past 30 years memorialization has increased in the form of monument-making and museum construction. A study by Paul Williams (2007) found that more memorial museums opened in the past 20 years than in the previous 100.

Liv Nilsson Stutz turns her attention to the growth of repatriation claims, and the global movement to return cultural heritage and human remains to minorities and indigenous populations. Claims for repatriation developed in North America and Australiasia in the 1980s and have spread to Britain and parts of Europe. Repatriation transfers human remains and objects that are considered to be in some sense affiliated to particular communities. The literature commonly interprets these movements and returns as positive and empowering. Repatriation is said to be a process of reconciliation and a strategy in which the communities of origin are said to regain the right to define themselves, their history and identity (see, for example, Fforde *et al.* 2002).

Nilsson Stutz is more questioning. She interrogates the contemporary theoretical foundations for the arguments that are used to support repatriation of cultural heritage. As with Viejo-Rose, Nilsson Stutz notes that the past is employed in these processes in constructing identity and that the appropriation of material culture, including monuments and artifacts, supports a political strategy for creating legitimacy and continuity through time. Repatriation movements rely on the idea that the human remains and cultural heritage of hundreds, if not thousands, of years ago belong to the descendants of the people that once produced them and only they, it is argued, can decide their fate. Further, it is argued that because of the past–present continuity that provides a crucial link between a contemporary group and a historical past in which an object was created, a particular contemporary group has a better understanding and insight into the object and its history. Nilsson Stutz draws attention to the problems associated with these assumptions, suggesting that if archaeology continues to reproduce this idea it may alienate us from the contemporary world characterized by a mix of identities, including migrants, hybrid and diaspora cultures. Problematically, she outlines, these arguments reproduce notions of past–present continuity, exclusive ownership of the past and of cultural heritage, underpinned by difference and essentialism—concepts that when they previously took a different form were rightly critiqued in post-colonial anthropological and archaeological theory. She argues that, although the repatriation process has positively democratized the production of knowledge about the past, in the sense that it has given the opportunity for more people and groups to participate in knowledge production, this process has placed restrictions on knowledge because certain groups are given a veto, or their voice is considered to be more important than scholarship.

Brian Hole turns to the role of heritage in nation-building in India, a large and diverse multination state that is constantly faced with the challenge of maintaining its unity. Hole looks at how concepts of an Indian nation have arisen, and at the state of Indian nationalism today. He then reviews the work of archaeologists and historians who have been involved with nationalist theories and movements and what their impact has been. In particular, Hole examines how, in the past two decades, the Hindu nationalist movement has become a significant factor in Indian politics, and has systematically leveraged heritage to create communal tensions. Hole argues that the use and interpretation of heritage plays a highly significant role and will thus directly help to determine the future form of the Indian nation-state. Looking to the future, he assesses the potential for Indian archaeology to counter right-wing nationalism, along with the potential internal and international consequences if it does not choose this path. Hole concludes by arguing that archaeologists and historians have a chance to play a very important role in determining the future of the Indian state, and of other states in the region. With Hindu nationalism posing a serious threat to stability and not showing signs of decline, he urges the establishment of an effective opposition to it, which needs to not only include the production of well-balanced research, but must also carefully refute nationalist misinformation and public education, he posits.

These are timely contributions. Heritage is too often considered in terms of how tourism might contribute to the economy post-conflict, neglecting the construction of meaning and memory through decisions about what is or is not preserved. There are a number of strands of thought raised by these articles that should stimulate further thinking. One rich vein is the impact on the people when culture is decided on and maintained by outside agencies. Charlotte Joy (2012) has scrutinized how the politics of heritage management plays an essential role in the construction of the past of the UNESCO World Heritage Site of Djenné and its inhabitants for contemporary purposes. Despite the global recognition of the significance of the site, the majority of local residents remain very poor. They may take pride in this heritage but they are troubled by the very real limitations it places on their day-to-day living conditions. Williams (2009) observed a similar problem at play in Brasilia, where, under UNESCO restrictions, people are unable to make changes to their living environment which would make it considerably safer to live in. In this instance, he says, UNESCO has prioritized heritage over the people.

Viejo-Rose and Hole suggest that building up cultural policies and strengthening the heritage sector through training and resources that take into account the post-conflict realities early in the process are essential to fomenting agency and accountability mechanisms for local professionals. These may be one way, but it is still important to ask what motivates these interventions, or rather, as Ibreck starts to probe, what is their underlying dynamic and how do these interventions benefit such external or international agencies? These are questions that are all the more urgent because the international community is becoming increasingly involved in the restoration and safeguarding of cultural heritage in societies marked by recent conflicts, including Cambodia, the former Yugoslavia, East Timor, Iraq and Afghanistan. In the case of Iraq, cultural professionals worked alongside the army, in an 'embedded' relationship, to seek to stem looting and the destruction of heritage sites. This may be a laudable aim, but it is one that is problematic due to the relationship between the intervening army and the profession. It is difficult to see how the heritage practitioner can be considered separate or distant from a military intervention when they are working alongside the army, occupying a country and—in this instance—its heritage.[2]

The repatriation of human remains and objects is an area where critical scrutiny of the process is notably absent. Nilsson Stutz helps to open this field up for further exploration. Other work has also started to do this by examining the role the museum profession has played in promoting this problem and how this grants them legitimacy in the context of a crisis of purpose (Jenkins 2010). A further area that requires consideration in relation to this subject and heritage projects more broadly, is the question of what vision of the human being is at their centre? Nilsson Stutz draws attention to the reconstruction of an essentialized racial or ethnic identity, and the problems with this. Neglected thus far is an examination of the therapeutic conception of the human person—in particular in relation to indigenous communities. The arguments for repatriation have tended to suggest that the process can bring about 'closure' and make amends for historical wrongs, that communities today are suffering from the impact of settler society and colonization, which can be alleviated by the repatriation of human remains (see, for example, Thornton 2002). This assumption is backed up by little—if any—evidence of this beneficial impact and warrants interrogation and research, for it is important to see this development as historically situated. John Torpey has argued that the turn towards a surge in reparations is due to the failure of certain movements to achieve material and political change, outlining that efforts to rectify past wrongs have arisen in part as a substitute for expansive visions of an alternative human future of the kind that animated the left-wing movements of the preceding century, and which have been overwhelmingly discredited. Inherently backward looking, with an idea of the beneficiary as vulnerable and in need of support, reparations politics may not be in the interests of these communities, despite their claims (Torpey 2006). It certainly helps to legitimize those agencies and states involved in making those reparations.

As these contributors highlight, there are serious questions to pursue about the globalization of international actors intervening in the heritage and culture of countries and peoples. Why are they intervening and what is the impact? Whilst these questions have always been important, the increased attention on heritage and culture, and the role they are assigned in the contemporary period, gives them urgency. I hope that these articles will contribute to opening up further discussion.

Notes

1 Convention for the Safeguarding of the Intangible Cultural Heritage (2003), p. 2.
2 See *Papers from the Institute of Archaeology* Vol. 19 (2009), for a debate on 'embedded archaeology'.

References

Fforde, C., Hubert, J. and Turnbull, P., eds, 2002. *The dead and their possessions: repatriation in principle, policy and practice.* London/New York: Routledge.

Jenkins, T., 2010. *Contesting human remains in museum collections: the crisis of cultural authority.* New York/London: Routledge.

Joy, C., 2012. *The politics of heritage management in Mali: from UNESCO to Djenné.* Critical Cultural Heritage Series. London: UCL Institute of Archaeology Publications.

Thornton, R., 2002. Repatriation as healing the wounds of the trauma of history: cases of Native America in the United States of America. *In*: C. Fforde, J. Hubert and P. Turnbull, eds. *The dead and their possessions: repatriation in principle, policy and practice.* London/New York: Routledge.

Torpey, J., 2006. *Making whole what has been smashed: on reparations politics.* Harvard University Press.

Williams, P., 2007. *Memorial museums: the global rush to commemorate atrocities.* Oxford: Berg.

Williams, R.J., 2009. *Brazil: modern architectures in history.* London: Reaktion Books.

Reconstructing Heritage in the Aftermath of Civil War: Re-Visioning the Nation and the Implications of International Involvement

Dacia Viejo-Rose

Culture is an indispensable asset in post-conflict recovery processes; however, it can also be used as a means of continuing violence on a symbolic and ideological level, particularly in the case of civil wars. In a reconstruction paradigm this violence often takes the form of struggles over history, memory, heritage, and identity. Despite the context-specific differences of conflicts, their aftermaths do retain some common elements—such as an emphasis on re-envisioning history and re-defining national identity. This article examines three issues: the intentionality guiding choices about what to rebuild, the symbolic landscape that emerges as a result, and the ethical issues that arise from third party intervention in the reconstruction of cultural heritage. The rhetoric that surrounds reconstruction projects differs widely from the reality on the ground and I will argue that it is important to understand this in order to assess the impact that reconstruction can have on attempts at reconciliation, identity and state-building. This article also examines some of the ethical issues involved in the post-conflict reconstruction of cultural heritage including the role of international values associated to 'heritage of mankind' and their possible conflict with local valuations of cultural heritage. This area of study is becoming increasingly urgent. International organizations have escalated their involvement in post-conflict reconstruction work and in these interventions they impress their particular code of values on fragile societies often without a full appreciation of the possible long-term consequences of their actions.

States develop their policy towards cultural heritage on the basis of a value framework that informs decisions about what remains of the past are worth preserving. The sites selected for preservation are in turn woven into a meta-narrative to construct a sense of national cohesion and history. Moments of acute crisis within societies, such as those presented by civil wars, cause radical shifts in these meta-narratives. The Human Development Report of 2005 shows that since the 1950s internal conflicts have been by far the most recurrent type. It is significant that civil wars require complex peace-building operations, particularly when previously warring sides are called on to collaborate in the process. This tendency has sparked a corresponding trend in international interventions; as Roland Paris (2004, p. 3) indicates, between 1989 and 1999, 14 major peace-building operations run by the United Nations (UN) were in countries that had experienced 'civil conflicts' and this trend has continued into the new century. Whether they involve contests for power between competing forces, the breaking up of states, irredentist or self-determination struggles, internal conflicts create divisions that can quickly become perceived as fathomless chasms. New narratives of difference are spun so that neighbours, colleagues, friends and even members of the same family find themselves on opposing sides of the conflict.

In the aftermath of such conflicts there is a rush to redefine the emerging state and its citizens. The foundational myths and narratives of a shared past and common destiny are submitted to revision and the boundaries of belonging and otherness shift like tectonic plates, destroying social networks, transforming the symbolic landscape and heritagescape.[1] This gives rise to significant challenges when the time comes to pick up the pieces and build up communities once again. It raises many questions: should reconstruction occur along the fault lines created by the conflict? Is the aim to return the country to its pre-conflict appearance? Is reconstruction an opportunity to redraw the politics of space and delimit new boundaries of inclusion and exclusion? What narratives of shared past and group belonging will be favoured and with what consequences?

The questions that arise from the complex scenario of reconstructing cultural heritage after civil wars will be discussed here in an attempt to identify and unpack the tiger traps, tools and trends of international involvement in such processes. When cultural heritage is considered in reconstruction projects, it is often in terms of how restoring an old town or heritage site will boost tourism, perceived as important in terms of both economic and social factors in the post-conflict economy and the process of 'normalization'. This view of the role of heritage reconstruction falls neatly into place within the predominant peace-building framework identified by Paris (2004, p. 5) for political and economic 'liberalization' through democratization and marketization respectively. Yet there is a danger in estimating the impact of cultural heritage reconstruction at this level alone, for the meaning and memories that it can evoke and transmit can be equally far reaching.

In the aftermath of war, heritage, more than ever, becomes a site of contestation and dissonance (Ashworth and Tunbridge 1996), both as a focus for conflicting interpretations of history and for the evaluation of the more recent conflict, its symbols and the new situation it engenders. This article argues that the reconstruction of heritage sites—by supporting an edited version of history, and by inscribing the emerging landscape with reminders of the war—constructs a revised vision, a revision, of the nation and redefines identities both within and outside its borders. As the international community becomes increasingly involved in the restoration and safeguarding of cultural heritage in societies marked by recent conflicts, such as Cambodia, the former Yugoslavia, East Timor, and Afghanistan, it is timely to look at some of the issues this raises. This international community comprises international governmental organizations (IGOs), such as the United Nations Educational, Scientific and Cultural Organisation (UNESCO), development agencies, diplomatic and cultural cooperation agencies, non-governmental organizations (NGOs), as well as a web of bilateral cooperation initiatives.

In this article, reconstruction is understood as a process that encompasses the restoration and rebuilding of some physical structures and building of new structures, as well as the parallel process of re-imagining the country's past, re-codifying its value system and formulating the resulting narratives. The shift in attitudes and values that a society undergoes as a result of conflict is reflected in choices concerning which heritage sites, historic moments or personages should be actively remembered and celebrated. The prime objective of reconstruction under study is the image and national narrative that is constructed by drawing on cultural heritage and subsequently projected internally to the state's citizens and externally to the international community. Internally this is carried out in a variety of ways: through school curricula and textbooks; through the public discourse projected by politicians, intellectuals, the media; through cultural policies, commemorations and festivities (public events and performances such as parades); through changes in street nomenclature; through the historical moments chosen to be celebrated or overlooked. Externally it is achieved through developing diplomatic relations, participating in international organizations and events (including sporting and cultural events such as the Olympics or World Fairs) and through the tourist industry, which is conducive to projecting a revised vision of the country.

This article examines two European wars that marked the first and second halves of the twentieth century: the Spanish Civil War of 1936–39 and the Bosnian War of 1992–95.[2] Despite the evident differences between the two conflicts there are some significant parallels: cultural heritage, its protection and destruction, was used in fierce propaganda battles and the international community became actively concerned with its fate. During the Spanish War the League of Nations and the International Office of Museums became involved in the Republic's efforts to safeguard the collection of Madrid's Prado Museum, which was eventually evacuated to Geneva for safekeeping in 1938. As a result of the propaganda battles in which both the Government of the Republic and the rebel military, calling themselves *los Nacionales*, 'the Nationals', accused each other of wilfully destroying, endangering or even selling the national heritage, international experts were called in as observers.[3] In addition to diplomatic organizations and professionals, intellectuals and artists also became engaged with the war, rallying international public opinion and media interest at a moment when photojournalism was in its early stages. During the Yugoslav wars of the 1990s, international attention regarding the fate of the region's artistic patrimony was first sparked by the shelling of the historical city of Dubrovnik, a World Heritage Site, by the Yugoslav National Army (JNA) from October–December 1991, and subsequently by the siege of Sarajevo and numerous other towns of Bosnia and Herzegovina between 1992 and 1995. International and regional organizations such as the UN and the European Union (EU) became concerned with the war, but it was UNESCO and the Council of Europe that raised the alarm about the deliberate destruction of the region's cultural heritage and called for respect of the Hague Convention (1954), particularly after the shelling of the Mostar bridge in November 1993—the Ottoman period (1566) bridge that gave the city its name. Internationally, intellectuals and artists also became involved in the conflict—with Susan Sontag famously staging *Waiting for Godot* in a besieged Sarajevo in 1993—at a moment when the use of the internet as a means of mass communication was in its early stages.

In both conflicts international attention was drawn to particular sites or actions. In Spain the aerial bombardment of the Basque town of Gernika (1937)—memorialized in Picasso's painting *Guernica*—and the killing of the poet Federico García Lorca (1936) are among such instances. In Bosnia, the principal cases were the massacre at Srebrenica, the destruction of the Mostar bridge and the siege of Sarajevo. The Spanish and Bosnian wars ended very differently. While in Spain the military rebellion, with the aid of its international allies, managed to defeat the Republic, in Bosnia the end of the fighting was achieved through the intervention of the UN and NATO (North Atlantic Treaty Organization): the Dayton Peace Accords (General Framework Agreement for Peace in Bosnia and Herzegovina, 14 December 1995) were brokered with the involvement of the United States, the European Union and Russia. In Spain one side came out of the conflict with a military victory, but this was not the case in Bosnia where fighting only ended as a result of outside intervention. The immediate post-war periods were therefore very different in the two cases, with a victorious side able to determine the shape of the reconstruction in the first and a process heavily driven by foreign intervention in the second. These differing results are significant because they determine who has the power and legitimacy to assign guilt, to construct the memory of the conflict and to readjust the boundaries that define the collective. Again, despite the differences between the Spanish and Bosnian experiences, there are shared implications. For instance, in both cases the silencing of guns did not end the violence or the destruction, which continued in different forms. Through identifying the common dynamics of these two conflicts in terms of how heritage was regarded and treated in contrast to the significant differences in the circumstances in which the subsequent reconstructions were carried out, this article seeks to examine the nation-building dimensions of reconstructing heritage after civil wars and the pros and cons of international involvement in that process.

Re-Visioning the Nation[4]

One domain of statebuilding played out in the reconstruction is the visual representation of the nation,[5] its past and its identity: new images arise out of the ruins, and old ones are re-envisioned. As part of the historical record, works of a society's cultural heritage are liable to be manipulated as they are preserved, exhibited or destroyed. Despite the context-specific differences of civil conflicts, their aftermaths do retain some common elements—such as an emphasis on re-inventing tradition and re-envisioning history, a form of historical territorialism in which there is little place for dialogue and reconciliation. History and heritage are represented in new ways as the nation's identity is tested, split apart and ultimately redefined.

This reconceptualized vision of the country, its past and its people is supported by an à la carte selection from the past; some historical moments are glorified while others disappear from the public sphere. As new historical sites, narratives, legends and myths become emphasized, so a new heritagescape emerges to support the re-visioned nation. The historical periods selected to mythologize as direct predecessors redraw an ancestral lineage. They then serve as guidelines for the visual construction of the newly defined nation while simultaneously providing the substance for a nationalist narrative and for making meaning through the association of values derived from that selection. Inevitably these narratives also redefine notions of otherness, excluding groups that once formed part of the nation.

Rebuilding the State, Re-Visioning the Nation: The Case of Spain

The Spanish Civil War began in July 1936 with an attempted military coup against the democratically elected government of the Second Republic. The coup failed and three years of civil war ensued during which the Spanish population, landscape, architecture, art collections and heritage sites suffered displacement and destruction. The targeting of church property at the start of the war and aerial bombardments throughout the war all had devastating effects. Yet, this material damage did not constitute the greatest violence waged on Spain's heritage; this was done by the propaganda war. At the beginning of the conflict officials on both sides often referred to the same national myths and historical moments in their rallying speeches. As the war continued, however, two opposing visions of Spain were hammered out, each representing the other as 'alien'. On this front, entire swaths of Spain's past were felled and large sections of the Spanish population disinherited from their past and their culture (Viejo-Rose 2011). The roots of the reconstruction that was to follow, particularly its cultural aspects, are to be found in the destructive effects of this wartime representation of the enemy other.

Already in January 1938, 14 months before the war ended, the insurgent military officers set up their first government in Burgos, with General Franco at its head. This government included a Service for Devastated Regions and Reparations (*Servicio de Regiones Devastadas y Reparaciones*) as well as a Service for the Defence of the National Artistic Patrimony (*Servicio de Defensa del Patrimonio Artístico Nacional*, PAN). The first of these services was set up under the auspices of the Ministry of Interior and at the end of the war it was upgraded to a General Directorate that worked in conjunction with the General Directorate for Architecture, the General Directorate for the Arts, and in collaboration with various instruments of the Spanish Falange, especially those sections in charge of press, propaganda and public acts. Through these bodies, all of which had regional nuclei but remained tightly monitored by the central offices in Madrid, the Franco regime sought to firmly control the reconstruction of Spain's heritagescape (Viejo-Rose 2009).

Yet, despite the privileged control exercised through the dictatorial power of the regime, there were discrepancies even at the level of rhetoric. The most salient divergence was that generated between a line of discourse which emphasized that the regime was restoring Spain to its 'authentic' values, traditions and place in the world, paralleled with another that placed the accent firmly on renewal and improvement. Furthermore, despite efforts at representing a unified front, the various groups constituting the regime's sphere of power—principally the Falange, Military, Church, Traditionalists, and Carlists—all had varying visions of the physical and moral shape that the country should take. The result was that each group tended to support different architectural and urban planning styles and had different perspectives on what should be restored or modernized. In addition to these discrepancies at the level of discourse, the gap between the grandiose plans for reconstruction projects on paper and the actual projects on site shape and pace of reconstruction grew progressively wider. There were three main reasons for this gap between the rhetoric and the reality of the reconstruction. One was the onset of World War II, which caused strategic materials—such as metals—to be scarce and difficult to obtain. Then there was the human toll that the war had taken on the Spanish population between the dead, wounded, displaced, imprisoned and exiled. Another reason was the excessive grandiosity of some of the original plans.

The reconstruction projects planned, projected and initiated from 1940 were largely finalized in the 1950s. Gradually, the inaugurations of completed reconstructions were replaced by inaugurations of large public works in the 1960s. The improvement of relations with the United States during these decades coupled with the desire to attract foreign tourists and investments led to a presentation of cultural heritage that sought to cater to expectations.[6] By 1975, when Franco died, 36 years of dictatorship had left a mark on the country's heritage, selectively celebrating or obscuring, restoring or neglecting, and creating a heritage of its own. The psychiatrist González Duro (2005) has analysed the far-reaching impact that both the war and the dictatorship had on the mental health of Spaniards, on their ability to mourn the losses of this period, and also on structures of governance in Spain, its political institutions and social attitudes to power. He makes the case that the political transition to a constitutional monarchy and democracy were strongly influenced by Francoist political culture, providing a great deal of continuity rather than offering a radical break and re-visioning of a democratic Spain.

Nearly 70 years after the end of the Civil War, José Luis Rodríguez Zapatero's government initiated a move to unearth what the construction of the New Spain had buried. The year 2006 was declared the 'Year for the Recovery of the Historic Memory', marking an important shift in how Spain now deals with the history of the Civil War and the Franco period. The government also insisted on legislating this process by creating the 'Law of the Historic Memory'.[7] There are two main elements to this law. The first addresses victimhood by recognizing victims on both sides of the civil war, as well as the victims of the Franco regime, and creates an administrative framework for supporting the excavation of unmarked and mass graves. The second deals with symbols, and legislates the removal of all material remnants of the Franco regime from public places (of statues, commemorative plaques, inscriptions and street names). These initiatives have spurred a heated political debate and the opposition party, the rightist *Partido Popular*, has protested vociferously, leading some commentators to remark that the battle lines of the civil war were emerging once again—suggesting that they had never fully disappeared (Viejo Rose 2011). Heated debates have been generated in Spain about the civil war dead—what to do with mass unmarked graves or with the *Valle de los Caídos*—and in 2006 there was a 'battle of obituaries' commemorating deaths from the 1930s that resuscitated the vocabulary of the period: *hordas rojas* and *bandas fasciosas*. One of these longstanding debates has revolved around the poet Federico García Lorca. In 2009, family members of the three men believed to have been buried with Lorca used the provisions of the new law to force the excavation of the burial site near Granada. In December 2009 a team of forensic archaeologists excavated the site where for many years people have gone on pilgrimages, deposited flowers, carried out commemorations, and where a monument to the poet was built. No human remains were found on the site. Lorca's family had long resisted the excavation, one of the arguments being that the important symbolism of the site might be overshadowed. Knowledge of the details, they argued, would detract from the timeless, international symbol of the poet's death—his silencing. It remains to be seen what the impact will be on the site of not having found the poet.

Reconstruction of Cultural Heritage in Bosnia and Herzegovina

One of the first signs of the breakdown of the former Yugoslavia was the resurgence of resentment and accusations relating to events of World War II. Despite the 40 years during which Tito's regime made considerable efforts to sweep aside the crimes of this war in the name of a unified brotherhood of Slavs, they had not been forgotten. Both Tudjman in Croatia and Milosevic in Serbia made inflammatory speeches about past battles and injustices, thus constructing the enemy 'other', portrayed as an imminent aggressive threat.[8] Throughout the wars that tore through the region for the most part of the 1990s the demonization of the enemy other continued, with international media coverage doing little to abate the trend. Despite the evident geopolitical and *real politik* motivations underlying the wars, those motivations took on the shape of ethnic violence. This was particularly apparent in Bosnia and Herzegovina, where the largely integrated heterogeneous society was split apart along ethnic and religious boundaries that came to define enemy lines. Society was thus fragmented into radicalized units defined largely by the manifestations of the newly essentialized differentials.

A cessation of the conflict was enforced by international intervention and international actors mediated the terms of the peace and developed the reconstruction programme. With regard to cultural heritage, the international community was active early on in reconstruction projects largely wrapped in a rhetoric proclaiming the merits of intercultural and inter-religious societies, cultural diversity and the dialogue of civilizations. Such idealistic visions, however, were often contradicted by those actually being forged by local reconstruction initiatives.

On 9 November 1993 the Stari Most crumbled into the waters of the Neretva after being the direct, deliberate target of shelling. Occurring some 19 months into a war that had thrown many neighbours, colleagues, friends and families onto opposite sides, the images of this bridge collapsing moved some to cry for the first time (Balic 2004). In this conflict that redrew and entrenched boundaries of difference and belonging, and which was permeated by a discourse of ethnic, religious and cultural antagonism, the collapse of the bridge was interpreted as a symbol of the ultimate collapse of dialogue and of a shared heritage. This act of wilful destruction, following after many others, seemed to resonate with particular force not only among Bosnians but also abroad. As such it became one of a series of acts that were to become landmarks of the wartime and post-war landscape. Partly for this reason, the international community directed attention and poured funds into rebuilding the bridge—a project loaded with the obvious metaphorical and literal message of reconnecting the two sides of this divided city. Yet, rebuilding the Mostar bridge has not been successful in reconstructing, by extension, the links of trust and communication between the town's communities. Mostar is perhaps the most divided city in Bosia and Herzegovina today (Bell 2010), with segregated schooling, two football teams (Zrinjski supported by Croats and Velež supported mostly by Bosniaks) and two universities (Sveučilište u Mostaru and Džemal Bijedić) in a city with an estimated population of 128,448. Not only are the Bosniak and Croat communities not integrating smoothly, but the Serb community has been returning very slowly. Furthermore, the circumstances of the bridge's destruction—by Croatian troops during the war—and the context of the reconstruction—by the international community—have added further symbolic dimensions to the site. While inter-national attention and resources focused on the reconstruction of the famous bridge, local communities were looking towards other sources and sites of symbolic meaning. In 2004, a local artist erected a bronze statue in honour of the Kung-fu legend Bruce Lee. In the words of one local: 'Lee is an international hero to all ethnicities in Bosnia and that's why we picked him' (Writer Veselin Gatalo quoted in BBC News 2004). This artistic intervention is eloquent in raising issues about those 'common symbols' that the international community was bent on finding and highlighting. It was also a commentary on a history ridden with confrontations in which the 'safe' shared symbols are those of international pop culture not necessarily those of world heritage.

The international community mobilized itself to reconstruct key symbolic buildings of the Catholic, Muslim and Orthodox communities in order to support its discourse of seeking to restore intercultural dialogue and community. For example, in Sarajevo, a city whose architecture reflects its diversity, a programme was undertaken to reconstruct and restore the Orthodox church (circa 1539), Roman Catholic cathedral (1889), Gazi Husrev Beg mosque (1531) and Sephardic synagogue (circa 1581). This project was presented as restoring Sarajevo's unique multicultural and inter-religious fabric. Yet, at the same time, also in Sarajevo, construction and reconstruction projects were being undertaken that fit less comfortably within a discourse of reconciliation, as old religious buildings continued to be razed and new ones erected. The King Fahd mosque, funded by Saudi Arabia, and the Istiqlal mosque, funded by Indonesia, are two cases of new mosques being built in Sarajevo that depart considerably from the traditional Ottoman style of Bosnian mosques. The King Fahd mosque is the biggest in the city, built largely in concrete, with loud speakers affixed to its minarets to announce the call to prayer. It is situated centre stage to the natural amphitheatre of the Serbian neighbourhood created by the geography of the river valley. More than restoring heritage these constructions are about demarcating space, and similar instances are echoed throughout the region with the construction of a modern Catholic church with a large bell tower in Mostar, or the construction of an imposing Orthodox church in Banja Luka. Rebuilding the more symbolic religious buildings in Sarajevo's old town was a necessary and valuable effort; however, it did not address the readings of their symbolism that had led to their initial targeting and which continued to fuel the destruction of religious buildings throughout Bosnia well after the Dayton Accords of 1995 (Wenzel 2001). There are other aspects of this dichotomy. While the international community focused on heritage sites of world renown, monuments to the partisan struggle of World War II that Tito had erected all around the former Yugoslavia were being torn down and neglected (Klaić 2002) while other important sites were being overlooked, such as the Bridge at Višegrad, the subject of the Nobel Prize for literature winning Ivo Andric's novel *The Bridge Over the Drina*.[9]

As in Spain, the rhetoric that surrounded reconstruction projects differed from the reality on the ground and came into conflict with local valuation of cultural heritage and perceptions of victim and perpetrator. In analysing the psychosocial healing of communities in the aftermath of civil war, Kimberly Maynard (in Kumar 1997, p. 210) identified five phases: establishing safety, communalization and bereavement, rebuilding trust and the capacity to trust, re-establishing personal and social morality, reintegrating and restoring democratic discourse. Cultural heritage is relevant in several of these phases. If symbolic sites continue to be destroyed and targeted even after the war has officially ended, as they were in Bosnia and Spain, a sense of safety will be difficult to establish. If grieving families of the dead, wounded, ill, exiled and imprisoned are excluded from mourning rituals and memorial practices a sense of community will be undermined by perpetuating a form of violence. This climate is not conducive to rebuilding trust, and together with the imposition of a moral framework prescribed by the new regime it will not contribute to fostering civil society and democratic discourse, and might, on the contrary, breed resentment.

Reconstructing Identity

Post-crisis societies are often depicted by their governing bodies as presenting an opportunity to redefine the nation. The rhetoric that accompanies this approach relies on reconstructing a new vision of the nation based on the selection of historic events and a reinterpretation of them to construct legitimizing myths for the transitional and ensuing regimes, their ideologies and key figures. This explicitly brings issues of culture and identity to the political forefront. For example, in 1990, Croatia's Strategy of Development identified the responsibilities of the Ministry of Culture to include: 'de-ideologizing of culture' and 'establishment of priorities and a hierarchy of values' (Schramadei 1998). By the time the conflict had ended in 1996 the main priorities had become preserving cultural heritage and 're-creating the representational image of national cultural identity' (Schramadei 1998).

Moments of acute conflict and crisis within a society can have profoundly distorting effects on individual and group identities. One such recurrent distortion is the simplification of group identities, classifying them into distinct and discrete groups along an irreconcilable boundary of 'us' and 'them'. In this scenario, cultural heritage can both bond groups together by creating the illusion of homogeneity, leading to new and wider chasms with other groups as the image of the enemy becomes radicalized. This inevitably has important consequences in the subsequent reconstruction process. Arguably, in societies emerging from disasters the tendency for the bonding mechanism to overshadow the bridging dynamic can result in an excluding ethnocentrism. The reconstruction process can easily contribute to further entrenching of the differences, thereby perpetuating communal antagonisms rather than fomenting a reconciliatory process. One criticism of the implementation of the Dayton Peace Accords in Bosnia is that in consciously trying to create a balance of power, it has further cemented the differences between groups. (See the example of the reconstruction of heritage sites in Sarajevo cited above, and several authors including Schake (1999), Bevan (2001), Tzifakis (2007), Hoare (2007) and Bell (2010).)

Amartya Sen (2006) has argued against a 'choiceless singularity' of identity. He points to the divisive and violent connotations of such a system of categorization that contradicts the reality of diversity in individuals' affiliations and ways of interacting with one another. He makes a powerful case for recognition of plural identities and their complexity, arguing against the illusion of a choiceless identity by calling for the return of the choice factor into the identity equation. This approach can help inform reconstruction practice so that it does not cement sectarian hatreds born of a conflict. This is possible when, as Handler (1994, p. 27) has pointed out, 'social groups—taken at any level of analysis (local, regional, national, trans-national)—are now conceptualized in terms of ongoing processes of "construction" and "negotiation"'. Avruch (2002, p. 80) indicates that one thing to be avoided is the over-simplification, stereotyping and thinking of culture as prescriptive. In the former Yugoslavia there were initiatives coming out of civil society that sought to counter one-dimensional representations of identity. For example, in 1993, well before the war ended, the Centre for Cultural Decontamination (CZKD, http://www.artfactories.net/CZKD-Center-For-Cultural.html) was set up in Belgrade in order to revive a 'liberal spirit of arts' and to create alternatives to the climate of nationalism and xenophobia that the war had engendered.

Memorials

Wars not only destroy heritage, they also spur the creation of new sites. Of these, memorials are perhaps the most tangible and widespread. War memorials are highly selective in terms of what and how they portray what is to be remembered (Rowlands 2011, King 2001). The construction of war heritage through memorials often gives preference to one group or version of events, to the detriment of others. Memorial plaques appeared all over Spain at the end of the war, on the facades of churches, town halls, in main squares and on monuments. They were marked by the exclamation '*¡Presentes!*' (Present!) and the slogan '*Caídos por Dios y por España*' (Fallen for God and for Spain) and listed the names of those men on the Nationalist side killed during the war. The names on these plaques indicated those who were supposed to be remembered, while those names absent from the plaques were intended to be forgotten. Paradoxically, the plaques served as mementos for the family members of those un-named in the memorials, mementos not only of their loss during the war but also of the injustice of the post-war. The memorials thus perpetuated the dichotomy between the victorious and the defeated. While the defeated could not build memorials in Spain to contest the official ones, this did not stop practices of mourning, commemoration and memorialization from taking place within the private sphere or by exiled communities. This process is clearly traceable in the case of Gernika; not only was the bombing commemorated in exile, but the painting became a form of memorial that powerfully contested the official ones. Since Franco's death, numerous memorials have been built to commemorate the experiences and loss of life on the Republican side during the war as well as that of the victims of the repression that followed. This demonstrates a need for public commemoration even 70 years, and two generations, after the war.

The contested character of memorials is also evidenced by how often they are targeted: public images of Franco and the memorial plaques of the regime were often the subject of vandalism and graffiti. In the context of a different dispute, the destruction of Nelson's pillar in Dublin by an IRA bomb in 1966 provides another example of the potentially antagonizing nature of public monuments. The ability of memorials to perpetuate division within society can also be seen in Bosnia where the Srebrenica-Potočari Memorial and Cemetery to Genocide Victims, inaugurated in 2003, on the site where several thousand Bosnian men were massacred in July 1995 has been the target of an attempted attack (*BBC News* 2003, Prevent Genocide International). Furthermore, parallel memorials commemorating the deaths of Bosnian-Serbs have emerged throughout the villages of this area, which is today part of Republika Srpska, such as in Kravica (Sahovic and Armakolas forthcoming). Memorial policies communicate messages about who, ultimately, has the right to mourn and be mourned, about who is to be remembered or not. Furthermore, the 'battles' of obituaries or memorials in which each side depicts itself as the greater victim can lead to competition for victimhood and for the moral victory that is perceived to come with it. This is especially so in the case of wars in which international public opinion is key and propagandistic attempts to sway it fierce. This was the case in both the Spanish Civil War and the Bosnian wars of the 1990s and is also the case with other conflicts such as that between Israel and Palestine.

Reconstruction inescapably occurs along the fault-lines created by the conflict, a scenario in which the politics of space, boundaries of inclusion and exclusion, have shifted or been emphasized. Civil war, that uncivil destroyer of cultural heritage which brings undercurrents of reproach, resentment and mistrust to the surface, has a long-lasting impact on the societies that suffer it. In the process of reconstruction, new regimes seek to lay claim to symbolic territory, imbuing sites with new meaning, constructing a narrative of the past and of the war, adjudicating guilt and responsibility for the destruction occasioned during the war. This process reaches into the past but its implications are in the present and the future, guiding policy decisions, attitudes and helping to shape state institutions. The work of Navaro Yashin (2002, 2010) is revealing of the lasting impact of population exchanges between Turkey and Greece and the relationship between those populations and the landscape and houses of the 'other' that they come to inhabit.

In this light, interventions that address culture and cultural heritage issues would not seem to be extravagant luxuries, despite the urgency of attending to many pressing basic human needs such as security, housing and employment. The values that inform the rebuilding of heritage sites will also inform the construction of infrastructures, state institutions, a judiciary and police force, and other dimensions of civic life. Seeing how these values are manifest in making decisions over one of these dimensions will help understand their impact on the others. Attitudes towards the past and choices about what moments of that past are to be cherished and celebrated can be exceptionally revealing. Examining these choices will contribute to determining how the divisions born of the conflict itself will shape the emergent state and society. Understanding the dynamics that drive the reconstruction of cultural heritage can thus be revealing as a statebuilding activity and could potentially be a valuable indicator of dysfunctional and failing states.

The Tools and Tiger Traps of International Involvement

As we have seen, the international community can find itself in situations in which it is rebuilding heritage—and through it symbols and narratives—that tells a very different story from the one that local communities build in parallel. The discrepancies between these visions are important to study in order to help understand just what role heritage does play. It is also in this difference that the involvement of international organizations can be constructive by providing assistance in the form of institution building and training rather than focusing on the reconstruction of iconic sites. For while the iconic sites may provide attractive photo opportunities they are also complex in the meanings and memories that they convey and their reconstruction can send messages that the international bodies involved the process did not intend.[10] While the international community has gradually begun adopting more long-term visions for their post-conflict interventions in the heritage domain a short-term perspective still lingers, particularly in terms of considering the longer term impacts, both intended and unintended. For, while the reconstruction of a site might take a few years, the impact of that site on the heritagescape lasts far longer and so should its management and integration into a larger framework. In the same way as building schools after a conflict needs to be accompanied by the development of curricula, textbooks and teacher training, when (re)building material heritage its immaterial dimensions should also be considered. Avruch (2002) provides an insightful word of warning:

> Given the varied roles that culture plays in conflict, it would seem that any practitioner entering a conflict situation in some other culture with an eye toward transformation or peace-building must have a formidable amount of substantive knowledge about the other culture: its key symbols, sacred signs, root metaphors, cognitive schemas, and worldviews, all of these embodied in a potentially 'foreign' language and wrapped, often contentiously, around competing versions of narrative history. (Avruch 2002, p. 79)

Building up cultural policies and strengthening the heritage sector through training and resources that take into account the post-conflict realities early in the process is essential to fomenting agency and accountability mechanisms for local professionals. In the long-run, this can be more conducive to developing responsible heritage management projects than one-offs in which international organizations parachute in with high profile iconic projects, while simultaneously local cultural entrepreneurs go about interpreting and managing the new landscape in their interests whether political or economic.

The heritagescape that is forged out of those sites that are chosen for reconstruction, preservation and celebration, conveys a message of power and legitimacy communicating the values and codes of conduct prioritized by the emerging regime. In Spain, a dictatorial regime sought to do this through a highly centralized and controlled reconstruction programme run by the Ministry of Interior. In Bosnia, the involvement of the international community in the form of

IGOs, NGOs, bi-lateral collaboration between countries, foundations, cultural cooperation bodies, professional associations, development agencies and religious groups resulted in a cacophony of voices. Each organization will have its own vision of the reconstruction, its own agendas and motivation for intervening (as in the case of Sarajevo mentioned above). Furthermore, their presence is often highly visible, for they stand out as foreigners, use identifiable vehicles such as black or white four-by-fours, set up work and living areas that are often characterized by barricades and high security, and often mark their spheres of action with large signs bearing the names or logos of the funding government or institution. This presence demarcates the terrain and the politics of space within it (Smirl 2008, pp. 236–253), adding a further symbolic layer to the physical, psychological and social ruins left by the war.

The attention awarded to a post-conflict scenario and the priorities identified are increasingly being shaped not by national but rather by international agendas and they need to be examined on this basis. Questions must be raised as to the ethics, the motives and the criteria behind the choices that initiate or sustain an international intervention in the reconstruction of cultural heritage after wars. Solidarity might in these circumstances distort agendas of national remembering, and the impact it can have on national narratives is inadequately understood. For instance, an intended impact of rebuilding the bridge in Mostar was to create a symbol of dialogue in a multicultural society, yet the city remains divided. The imposition of this prescriptive symbolic meaning on the bridge's rebuilding was not entirely successful. Among other things, the new bridge is a reminder of international involvement in the reconstruction. What are the tiger traps of international involvement? The ones that will be addressed here are the following: the positivist value often associated with heritage, the concept of universal value, the tension that exists between professional technical expertise and local ideological motivations, and the issue of timing.

Ingrained in the discourse that calls to protect cultural heritage and safeguard diversity is a positive moral vernacular which suggests that heritage is inherently 'good'. Yet, heritage can be made to convey violent and exclusionary messages and a society entrenched in its diversities might not be disposed to dialogue or open to multiple readings of that heritage. Ignoring the less benign interpretations of heritage neither addresses the factors that make it a target in the first place nor the possible messages that its reconstruction might send. As the study by Ashworth and Tunbridge (1996, p. 261) makes clear 'all heritage is dissonant to someone, and all dissonance is someone's heritage'. In 1919 John Maynard Keynes published *The Economic Consequences of Peace* as a commentary on the Treaty of Versailles that ended World War I, which, he argued, planted the seeds for a future war. This is a fundamental insight when considering the post-war reconstruction of heritage, which, like the terms of a peace treaty, can set the terrain for a future conflict. The problem of one-dimensional interpretations of heritage is that they are excluding and more apt to be used in constructing opposite, radical and equally one-dimensional narratives of group identity. In the aftermath of war, heritage more than ever becomes a site of contestation and dissonance (Ashworth and Tunbridge 1996), as both a focus for opposing interpretations of the conflict and the ensuing uses made of it. Only by recognizing this and dispelling the nomenclature that characterizes heritage as a container of exclusively positive values and narratives is it possible to understand it in the post-war context. Only by recognizing its potential to impart messages of fear, domination and violence can its potential as a resource in reconciliation be engaged and any historical grievances linked to it addressed (for the role of culture in peace-building and reconciliation see Galtung 1990, 1996, Lederach 1997, 1999). Yet, thus far, efforts of the international community to reconstruct heritage sites in war-torn countries have treated heritage as being an intrinsically positive value, something to be cherished, safeguarded and restored in the name of 'outstanding universal value' as set out in the Convention for the Protection of the World Cultural and Natural Heritage (UNESCO 1972), which is still the principal defining document for tangible, monumental heritage.[11] If the multiple facets and interpretations of heritage sites are not addressed initially, then the risk exists that through well-intentioned reconstruction projects aimed at reconciliation the opposite results could be reaped.

A dilemma that the notion of universal value brings up in the context of post-conflict reconstruction is that conflict precisely breaks social groups down into units determined by strong social ties, personal histories, and their related emotions, memories and communal loyalties (Kumar 1997). These distorted social groups with a tendency towards introversion and protectiveness will be reluctant to collaborate with other groups with whom all ties were broken during the conflict. A dichotomy arises between local valuations of heritage and the 'universal value' approach adopted in notions of world heritage. In an extremely polarized society, with individual and social collectives, social ties and communal networks still relating on the basis of their experiences and memories of the conflict, abstract notions of universal values seem to lose their strength and validity. Yet, conversely, this distance from the conflict and its abstraction makes it a useful concept in drawing attention away from vengeful sentiments towards what can be a common resource. The idea of 'universal value' when ascribed to heritage is increasingly being criticized, indicating its subjectivity, malleability and vulnerability to manipulation. It is nonetheless difficult to do away with it entirely and it is intimately intertwined with the World Heritage label, a basic instrument of international cooperation on heritage. The concept of universal value associated with world heritage can offer a point of access for post-conflict interventions that can thus claim to be pursuing a universal right, a human right. However, in order to be effective it cannot simply be imposed from above or used as rhetoric in which to package reconstruction projects. Its usefulness lies in its potential to bring a fractured community into dialogue to identify and safeguard sites that all groups recognize and value. Some international organizations have veered away from consultation in these circumstances because society is so divided and the demands made by the various groups when consulted often clash and seem counter to reconciliatory aims. The wars that ravaged the former Yugoslavia during the 1990s have set precedents with important consequences for cultural heritage. The attack of the Old Town of Dubrovnik (inscribed on the World Heritage List in 1979) drew particular attention because of its category as 'heritage of mankind' enforced by the fact that Yugoslavia had been one of the first state signatories of the World Heritage Convention. One of the most important outcomes of the shelling of Dubrovnik has been that the International Criminal Tribunal for the former Yugoslavia at the Hague found a Lieutenant-General guilty of 'destruction or wilful damage done to institutions dedicated to religion, charity and education, the arts and sciences, historic monuments and works of art and science, a violation of the laws or customs of war under Article 3 of the Statute' (ICTY 2005). This tribunal determined sites inscribed on this list to be deserving of particular protection by the international community (Francioni and Lenzerini 2008).

There are two trends of international cooperation on heritage reconstruction. The first relies on the provision and exchange of technical expertise. Conservation experts, art historians, architects, engineers and urban planners are mobilized either by professional organizations such as ICCROM, NGOs such as Architects Without Borders, foundations such as the Aga Khan Foundation for Islamic Heritage, or bilateral collaboration between museums, universities or even local governments through town-twinning programmes. The discourse that surrounds this form of international involvement is imbued with the language of scientific knowledge and technical expertise. This approach can be useful because it appears less threatening to state sovereignty, a kind of *Médecins Sans Frontières* for cultural heritage, going in to save monuments and sites from disappearing. This strength is also it weakness, for it fails to address the reasons behind the destruction and is thus liable to overlook the biases of reconstruction policies. The second trend tries to deal with this central issue. Yet it often comes laden with a system of values that is then imposed, fuelled by motivations such as building 'intercultural dialogue' or a 'culture of peace'. This approach attempts to tackle the 'whys' of the destruction and the reconstruction itself but often fails to go profoundly into the issues for fear of provoking further tensions. Nevertheless, sugar-coating reconciliatory discourse is not constructive, as it does not engage with the potential of using heritage sites to mediate diverse interpretations of heritage, memory and identity. Community-based reconstruction projects are one tool that relief and development specialists are trying to implement as a way of mitigating tensions indirectly and instilling collaboration. Implementing this approach in projects involving cultural heritage can involve consultation processes through which the image of the 'enemy other' constructed during the war can begin to be dissipated. In this process, focus could encompass the multiplicity of interpretations of heritage, allowing space for dialogue and joint decision-making that might begin to restore links between social groups, between citizens and their culture, between citizens and their past. Contradictorily, the foremost condition for a diversity of voices to be equally represented can also become a stumbling block when trying to reach some consensus over what to rebuild and how—as indicated by Mostar's Bruce Lee sculpture mentioned above. Attempts to impose a vision of heritage in post-civil war reconstructions have not been successful. As is evident in the cases of Spain and the former Yugoslavia, when a contested past is simply dropped from textbooks and the official version of history it nevertheless continues to be transmitted privately in communities and families. Regardless of whether the vision being imposed seeks to maintain the memory of the conflict and keep its divisions alive or on the contrary to establish intercultural dialogue and reconciliation, alternative interpretations persist and eventually resurge. This indicates a need to develop approaches that are more open to including a variety of voices even when some of these voices seemingly contradict the motivations of the main actors of the reconstruction. Given that one way of trying to reach a consensus is by looking outside the immediate context, then the notion of the universal value of heritage can here be applied to advantage.

Finally, there is the issue of time. The social and spatial topography of cities throughout Spain and Bosnia changed as a result of the wartime destruction and ensuing reconstruction, and so did their symbolic landscapes. The reconceptualized vision of the country and its people was supported by an á la carte selection of the past with some historical moments glorified while others disappeared from the public sphere. As new historical sites, narratives, legends and myths were emphasized, so a new heritagescape emerged to support the re-visioning of the nation. The historical periods chosen as direct precursors not only provided guidelines for the visual construction of the newly defined nation, they were also associated with particular values and visions of the nation's place in the world. Inevitably these narratives also redefined notions of otherness, excluding groups that once formed part of the nation. At best, hasty reconstructions fail to respect the wealth and depth of meanings and symbols that make cultural heritage so important to societies. In a worst case scenario these reconstructions can actually carry forth the violence and fear engendered by the conflict by acting as aggressive signposts and propelling a negative cycle of reconstruction (Figure 1) rather than a reconciliatory one. As a result of his experience as High-Representative for Bosnia and Herzegovina (2002–6), Paddy Ashdown (2007) has repeatedly called on the need to take more time over reconstruction projects and processes. This negative conflict cycle has been noted by others, for instance Collier *et al.* (2006) note that approximately half of all civil wars are the result of post-conflict relapses.

The post-conflict reconstruction of Spain and Bosnia were clearly very different in their protagonists, motivations, methods and intended outcomes. It is not the intention of this article to defend the thesis that the international community behaves in the same way as a dictatorial regime. By putting the two cases side-by-side, however, it is possible to discern some common trends in the reconstruction of cultural heritage as a process. Also, looking at the Spanish case, in which there was one dictatorial regime, albeit with its internal conflicts and contradictions, which was in charge of the reconstruction and remained in power for nearly 40 years, can provide a fruitful contrast with today's interventions characterized by a wide scope of actors and agendas precisely because identifying the vision for the reconstruction and tracing its medium-term impacts

POLITICAL CULTURE, SOFT INTERVENTIONS AND NATION BUILDING

Civil War

Heritage sites are shaped by the war, new ones created and old ones reinterpreted (e.g. sites of battles, massacres and victories)

Reconstruction begins with this transformed landscape as its foundation

Resentment and the transmission of a 'historical injustice' continue

The management of cultural heritage contributes to perpetuating violence and undermining reconciliation

Events, protagonists and ideologies of the conflict influence reconstruction policies and memorial practices

Reconstruction cements divisions—the re-valuation of heritage and the selection of commemorative events reinforce this trend

Figure 1. Negative cycle of cultural heritage reconstruction.

is possible. Further comparative research would be important in investigating the intentionality of reconstruction projects, the aims of intervening, the motivations that guide decisions about what to re-build and how, and the impact that these projects have on attempts at reconciliation, identity and statebuilding. An outline of some of the key dynamics of reconstruction, its aims, uses of the past, construction of new codes and outcomes is presented in Figure 2. What comes out most notably from this is that the reconstruction is guided by a desire to shape a value system, planting symbols in the landscape that will communicate it. The resulting heritagescape thus serves as a mnemonic device, a reminder of that value system which simultaneously transmits a message about power: for it is those with the economic and political power in a post-conflict scenario that will make decisions about priorities, about what to rebuild or not.

Understanding the long-term impact of reconstruction is one of the aims of the EU funded project Cultural Heritage and the Re-Construction of Identities after Conflict (CRIC, http://www.cric.arch.cam.ac.uk), which looks at the battlefields of post-World War I France, Dresden in the aftermath of World War II, Gernika and Spain's gradual reconstruction in the aftermath of the Civil War, Francoisim and the bombings of 11 March 2004, and also at Bosnia and Cyprus.

On a positive note, sites that have been targeted during conflicts can be remarkably resilient. Acts of destruction can come to have a resonance and symbolic capital that is transformed into a symbol of peace. Since the 50th anniversary commemoration in 1987 of the bombing of Gernika (26 April 1937), the town and its events and institutions have gradually included a discourse of peace. Gernika received the UNESCO Cities for Peace Prize (2002–3) and the museum of Gernika was re-inaugurated in 2003 as the Gernika Peace Museum and hosted the 2005 International Conference of Peace Museums. In parallel terms, in

POLITICAL CULTURE, SOFT INTERVENTIONS AND NATION BUILDING

Aims
- New regimes seek to centrally control the reconstruction, regardless of regional or local administrative branches, in order to establish, formalize and communicate a new structure of authority and power.
- Reconstruction seeks to establish order and legitimacy. It does this through urban planning policies which integrate or erase heritage sites and through presenting an edited version of history.

Uses of the past
- An edited version of history and memory is constructed to give legitimacy to the post-war administration.
- This version of history is reflected in many forms, including popular culture and school textbooks and curricula. It also guides decisions about what heritage sites to preserve or not.
- The constructed narrative of the past is reinforced through celebration and performance.
- The central analytic element in understanding the process of creating a selective past is that of choice. The choices that are made about what to celebrate and 'remember' and what to deliberately obfuscate and 'forget' reveal a set of motivations and intents behind the reconstruction project.
- The preferred historic legends of an inward looking regime will be those that emphasize heroism and sacrifice.

Re-codifying
- Codifying the past and mourning through the reconstruction: building memorials, commemorative practice and a selective use of the past.
- Post-war scenarios often see the emergence of moral effigies, archetypes constructed in a new mythology resulting from the conflict.
- These re-codify history, landscape and social behaviour.
- The image of the phoenix rising from the ashes gets used both to signify renovation and a new start and that the old will be restored to its past glory.

Outcomes
- Despite their aims, national reconstruction projects are rarely able to maintain close control over the process, partly due to a lack of resources, partly due to inevitable delays; there is a tendency for vast discrepancies to emerge between the rhetoric and the reality of reconstruction projects.
- Attempts to impose valuation frameworks either by a national authority or international agency rarely manage to stamp out a diversity of voices and alternative interpretations and memories are resilient and can re-emerge.

Figure 2. Towards a protocol: outline of key dynamics.

Mostar a Centre for Peace and Multiethnic Cooperation was created, which since 2004 has awarded a peace prize; all the prizes have gone to international figures.[12] In both instances, the moves towards peace symbolism began functioning on an international plane thanks in part to the renown of Picasso's painting *Guernica* in one case and in the other to the scale of reporting on the destruction of the bridge at Mostar, thus projecting these instances of destruction internationally. Furthermore, in Gernika, in recent years a parallel trend has emerged in which local organizations, including the museum, have gradually begun to include current regional and national conflicts into their peace-building work.

Concluding Remarks

Cultural heritage is an indispensable asset in post-conflict recovery processes; however, it can also be used as a means of continuing violence on a symbolic and ideological level, particularly in the case of civil wars. In a reconstruction paradigm this violence often takes the form of struggles over history, memory, heritage and identity as well as attempts to demarcate the past, present and future of the newly recovering society and state. Giving a tangible form to grief can become a reminder of the grievance, and while answers are not easily forthcoming, they must be sought through consultation with the affected communities and by means of greater interaction between researchers and practitioners. Despite the context-specific differences of distinct conflicts, their aftermaths do retain some common elements—such as an emphasis on re-envisioning history and re-defining national identity. The post-conflict situation can be seen as a dialectic in which the newly formed (or fragmented) state offers a vision to its citizens of their identity and heritage, and the citizens accept it, reject it or make a counter-offer.

This area of study is becoming increasingly urgent. International organizations have escalated their involvement in post-conflict reconstruction work and in these interventions they impress their particular code of values on fragile societies often without an understanding of the long-term consequences of their actions. Regardless of their intentions, an autocratic regime, a democratic government and an international organization will all rebuild according to a set of values, a conceptualization of the conflict (who were the victims and who the perpetrators), and an agenda (influenced by budgets, political manoeuvring and perceived time frame for action). These factors will impose a vision and rhythm on the reconstruction process, shaping policies and a methodology accordingly.

Reconstruction requires a series of choices in determining what sites of cultural heritage are to be rebuilt or abandoned; the narrative that binds these decisions together gives rise to a new value-scape. The decisions made on what elements of cultural heritage are rebuilt and how they are presented will effect the future development of meaning and symbols in the surrounding communities and will thus influence how they interact with the Other. The richness of a heritage site today is composed of the accumulation of all its past meanings, it is not, nor can ever be, 'neutral' and its meaning cannot be controlled or policed for dissonance. The tiger trap lies in one-dimensional interpretations of heritage that are necessarily exclusive and excluding and therefore more apt to produce radical narratives of group identity. The challenge is for reconstruction projects to incorporate spaces for a diversity of meanings and interpretations.

The legacy of history can be a heavy burden in the effort to move towards peace and stability. In instances when the destruction of cultural heritage has been heavily used for propaganda purposes in wartime rhetoric, the reconstruction process is delicate to say the least as memories of the destruction of cultural heritage can prolong fear and resentment. Cultural heritage is a cornerstone of the framework that is built up after a conflict because it is used to support a meta-narrative of the nation, its past, present and common destiny. Since cultural heritage quickly becomes mobilized as a bellicose instrument during conflicts it is equally important to begin 'disarming' it from the beginning rather than wait until it has once again become an antagonistic marker.

Acknowledgements

The author would like to thank Dzenan Sahovic at the University of Umeå for reading and commenting on an early draft of this article as well as her colleagues on the EU funded project Cultural Heritage and the Reconstruction of Identities after Conflict (CRIC, http://www.cric.arch.cam.ac.uk). Some of the ideas presented in this article were first introduced in Viejo-Rose (2007) and further examined in Viejo-Rose (2011).

Notes

1   Mary-Catherine Garden (2006) first used this term to refer to how heritage sites more and less successfully convey a sense of place. The use of the term in this article builds on a broader understanding of the term (Viejo Rose 2011) to include a sense of the multiplicity and malleability of symbolic meaning, interrelations and interpretations of heritage sites which are in a state of constant flux and imbue a landscape with a myriad of meanings.

2   There are dissenting definitions of what constitutes a civil war. Collier and Hoeffler (2001), Paris (2004) and Armitage (2008) consider Bosnia as a civil or internal war, though admittedly the wars that comprised the dissolution of Yugoslavia took different forms throughout their various stages, including secessionist and foreign aggression. What is important for the purpose of this study is the process by which a structure fragments and in so doing tears rifts through society, neighbourhoods and families.

3   Sir Frederic Kenyon, former Director of the British Museum, together with James Mann, Director of the Wallace Collection, visited Republican-held areas, and Michael W. Stewart of the Victoria and Albert Museum visited Nationalist-held territory in 1937.

4   'Re-visioning' here means how the idea of the nation is at once re-imagined and revised and how the resulting image is in turn visually represented both nationally and internationally.

POLITICAL CULTURE, SOFT INTERVENTIONS AND NATION BUILDING

5   Statebuilding here refers to the construction and stabilization of public institutions and structures such as those dedicated to governance and a judiciary while 'nation-building' refers to the formation of the body polity that the state structures should serve.

6   This is brilliantly captured in Luis García Berlanga's 1953 film *Bienvenido Mister Marshall*.

7   The official name of the law, approved in October 2007, is 'Ley por la que se reconocen y amplían derechos y se establecen medidas en favor de quienes padecieron persecución o violencia durante la Guerra Civil y la Dictadura'.

8   See Bet-El in Müller (2002) for references to Milosevic's use of the past. See Tanner (1997) for an appraisal of Tudjman's use of the past. Also Colovic's 'War Folklorism: Zagreb Lasses and Captain D' in Borden *et al.* (1992) and Hall (1994).

9   This bridge was inscribed on the World Heritage List in 2007 as the Mehmed Paša Sokolović Bridge in Višegrad; the old bridge area of the old city of Mostar was inscribed in 2005.

10   This links back to Paris's analysis of the ideologically liberal standards of the international community, but it is also important because of the number of religiously oriented interventions in heritage reconstruction with different countries or NGOs funding the religious group with which they have affiliations.

11   More recent normative instruments developed by UNESCO, such as the Convention for the Safeguarding of the Intangible Cultural Heritage (2003), acknowledge the importance of communities, groups and individuals in the valuation of heritage, the idea of 'universal value' continues to underlie the notion of world heritage which gets called on to justify interventions (i.e. Dubrovnik).

12   Vaclav Havel, ex-President of Czechoslovakia in 2004; Alois Mock, ex-Chancellor of Austria in 2005; Nelson Mandela, ex-President of South Africa in 2006; Mohammed Elbaradei, General Director of the International Atomic Energy Agency in 2007.

References

Armitage, D., 2008. *Civil war from Rome to Iraq*. Available from: http://www.abc.net.au/tv/fora/stories/2008/09/25/2362274.htm [Accessed 1 July 2009].

Ashdown, P., 2007. *Swords and ploughshares: bringing peace to the 21st century*. London: Weidenfeld and Nicolson.

Ashworth, G. and Tunbridge, J., 1996. *Dissonant heritage: the management of the past as a resource in conflict*. Chichester: John Wiley and Sons Ltd.

Avruch, K., 2002. What do I need to know about culture? A researcher says...' *In*: J.-P. Lederach and J. Moomaw, eds. *A handbook of international peacebuilding: into the eye of the storm*. San Francisco: Jossey-Bass, 75–88.

Balic, A., 2004. The new 'old bridge': a story from Mostar. *UN Chronicle*, Sept.–Nov.

BBC News, 2003. Clinton to open Srebrenica memorial, 4 Aug. Available from: http://news.bbc.co.uk/1/hi/world/europe/3123485.stm [Accessed 27 June 2009].

BBC News, 2004. Bruce Lee statue for Bosnian city, 2 Sept. Available from: http://news.bbc.co.uk/1/hi/entertainment/3620752.stm [Accessed 19 June 2009].

Bell, M., 2010. *The rise and fall of Yugoslavia: the story of Tito*. Episode 2. Radio, BBC4. 3 May.

Bet-el, I.R., 2002. Unimagined communities: the power of memory and conflict in the former Yugoslavia. *In*: J.-W. Müller, ed. *Memory and power in post-war Europe: studies in the presence of the past*. Cambridge: Cambridge University Press, 206–222.

Bevan, R., 2001. Bricks and mortars. *In*: *Bosnian report*. Bosnian Institute, 9 Oct. Available from: http://www.bosnia.org.uk/news/news_body.cfm?newsid=1558 [Accessed 5 May 2010].

Bienvenido Mister Marshall!, 1953. Film. Directed by Luis García Berlanga. Spain: Unión Industrial Cinematográfica (UNINCI).

Boutros-Ghali, B., 1992. *An agenda for peace: preventive diplomacy, peacemaking and peace-keeping*. New York: United Nations.

Collier, P. and Hoeffler, A., 2001. *Greed and grievance in civil war*. World Bank Working Paper 2355. Washington, DC: World Bank.

Collier, P., Hoeffler, A. and Söderbom, M., 2006. *Post-conflict risks*. CSAE WPS/2006-12. Oxford: University of Oxford, Centre for the Study of African Economies.

Colovic, I., 1992. War folklorism: Zagreb lasses and Captain D. *In*: A. Borden *et al.*, eds. *Breakdown: war and reconstruction in Yugoslavia, YUGOFAX—War report and the Helsinki Citizens Assembly*. London: Institute for War and Peace Reporting, 53–60.

Francioni, F. and Lenzerini, F., eds, 2008. *The 1972 World Heritage Convention. A commentary*. Oxford/New York: Oxford University Press.

Galtung, J., 1990. Cultural violence. *Journal of peace research*, 27 (3), 291–305.

Galtung, J., 1996. *Peace by peaceful means*. London: Sage.

Garden, M.-C., 2006. The heritagescape: looking at landscapes of the past. *International journal of heritage studies*, 12 (5), 394–411.

González Duro, E., 2005. *La sombre del General. Qué queda del franquismo en España*. Barcelona: Arena Abierta, Debate, Random House Mondadori.

Hall, B., 1994. *The impossible country: a journey through the last days of Yugoslavia*. New York: Penguin Books.

Handler, R., 1994. Is identity a useful cross-cultural concept? *In*: J.R. Gillis, ed. *Commemorations: the politics of national identity*. Princeton, NJ: Princeton University Press, 27–41.

Hoare, M.A., 2007. *The history of Bosnia: from the Middle Ages to the present day*. London: Saqi.

International Criminal Tribunal for the former Yugoslavia (ICTY), 2005. Judgement in the Case the Prosecutor v. Pavle Strugar. 31 January 2005, Court ruling: CT/P.I.S./932e. The Hague. Available from: http://www.icty.org/sid/8655.

Keynes, J.M., 1919. *The economic consequences of peace*. New York: Harcourt, Brace, and Howe, Inc.

King, A., 2001. Remembering and forgetting in the public memorials of the Great War. *In*: A. Forty and S. Küchler, eds. *The art of forgetting*. Oxford: Berg Publishers, 147–170.

Klaić, D., 2002. Enjeux de memoire: Franje, l'hospital des partisans [Contentious memory: Partisan Hospital Franje]. *Transeuropéennes*, (22), 270–274.

Kumar, K., ed., 1997. *Rebuilding societies after civil war: critical roles for international assistance*. Boulder, CO; London: L. Rienner.

Lederach, J.P., 1997. *Building peace: sustainable reconciliation in divided societies*. Washington DC: United States Institute of Peace Press.

Lederach, J.P., 1999. *The journey toward reconciliation*. Scottdale, PA: Herald Press.

Navaro-Yashin, Y., 2002. *Faces of the state: secularism and public life in Turkey*. Princeton, NJ: Princeton University Press.

Navaro-Yashin, Y., 2010. *The make-believe space: affect, law, and governance in an abjected territory*. Durham, NC: Duke University Press.

Paris, R., 2004. *At war's end: building peace after civil conflict*. Cambridge: Cambridge University Press.

Prevent Genocide International. Website last revised 24 May 2005. Available from: http://www.preventgenocide.org/edu/pastgenocides/formeryugoslavia/resources/ [Accessed 19 June 2009].

Rowlands, M., 2001. Remembering to forget: sublimation as sacrifice in war memorials. *In*: A. Forty and S. Küchler, eds. *The art of forgetting*. Oxford: Berg Publishers, 129–146.

Sahovic, D. and Armakolas, I. (forthcoming). Available from: http://www.cric.arch.cam. ac.uk/case-studies/bosnia.html.

POLITICAL CULTURE, SOFT INTERVENTIONS AND NATION BUILDING

Schake, K., 1999. The Dayton Peace Accords: success or failure? *In*: K.R. Spillmann and J. Krause, eds. *International security challenges in a changing world*. New York: Peter Lang, 281–295.

Schramadei, P., 1998. *Cultural policy database. Country profiles: Croatia*. Culturelink. Available from: http://www.culturelink.org/culpol/croatia.html [Accessed 9 May 2010].

Sen, A., 2006. *Identity and violence: the illusion of destiny*. London: Penguin Books.

Smirl, L., 2008. Building the other, constructing ourselves: spatial dimensions of international humanitarian response. *International political sociology*, 2, 236–253.

Tanner, M., 1997. *Croatia: a nation forged in war*. New Haven, CT: Yale University Press.

Tzifakis, N., 2007. The Bosnian peace process: the power-sharing approach revisited. *Perspectives. Review of international affairs*, 28 (2007), 85–102.

UNESCO, 1972. *Convention concerning the protection of the world cultural and natural heritage*. Paris: UNESCO.

Viejo-Rose, D., 2007. Conflict and the deliberate destruction of cultural heritage. *In*: Y.R. Isar and H. Anheier, eds. *Cultures and globalization: conflicts and tensions*. London: Sage, 102–116.

Viejo-Rose, D., 2011. *Reconstructing Spain: cultural heritage and memory after civil war*. Brighton: Sussex Academic Press.

Wenzel, M., 2001. Bosnia and Herzegovina: danger, through social readjustment, to cultural property which had survived war. *Museum management and curatorship*, 19 (3), 316–321.

International Constructions of National Memories: The Aims and Effects of Foreign Donors' Support for Genocide Remembrance in Rwanda

Rachel Ibreck

Commemoration of the victims of conflict is a characteristic national act of post-conflict statebuilding in which the significance and ownership of memorials is typically contested. In the case of post-genocide Rwanda, such contestation is overlain with international agendas and influences. Certain international donors supported memorialization as part of programmes to aid societal reconstruction and reconciliation and to prevent conflict. Studies of international contributions to genocide memorials, especially the Kigali Genocide Memorial Centre, reveal tensions in this agenda, which seeks to construct both national identity and an imagined 'international community' and serves to extend the remit of international actors.

In post-conflict arenas, international donors and non-governmental organizations (NGOs) now seek to repair not only physical infrastructure and the institutions of government, but society as well. They seek to 'rebuild' not only states but societies by addressing the legacies of the past, including the psycho-social effects of violence (Scheper-Hughes 2005, p. 166). In Rwanda, they sponsored a range of justice and reconciliation initiatives to promote recovery from the trauma of the 1994 genocide, including the development of genocide memorials. This unusual project illuminates the ambitions and approach of international donors and demonstrates the extent of their involvement in the re-imagining of Rwanda after the genocide. International engagement is penetrating the very fabric of national identity, encroaching on territory normally reserved for the most profound domestic political agendas.

The participation of international donors and NGOs in the construction of genocide memorials in Rwanda has special significance because public remembrance of conflict has typically been associated with the idea of the nation and driven by the priorities of the state. Violent deaths have been 'remembered/forgotten as our own' within the national political community (Anderson 1991, p. 206). The intimate connection between public memory and national identity emerged in the nineteenth century in Western nations (Gillis 1994, pp. 8–12) but became evident elsewhere as state elites in post-colonial nations promoted collective memories in order to construct legitimacy and hegemony (Davis 2005, Werbner 1998).

In post-genocide Rwanda the ruling party, the Rwandan Patriotic Front (RPF), has strategically used the platform of commemoration to promote a selective account of the past in support of its own political interests (Vidal 2001). Rwanda's genocide remembrance has been marked by a troubled relationship between the RPF agenda and the demands and activities of mainly Tutsi genocide survivors, the group that has a primary claim to the ownership of remembrance (Ibreck 2010). Many members of the ethnic Hutu majority also see memorialization as a mechanism for ascribing collective guilt and excluding them from political power (Lemarchand 2009). Such contests are familiar material to the historian of public remembrance.

The Rwanda case, however, also indicates how contemporary memorialization is shaped by international actors. It reflects a worldwide turn towards 'post-national' commemoration (Gillis 1994, p. 13), with the spread of an international human rights narrative and a shift towards the transnational production and dissemination of memories in the context of globalization (Ashplant *et al.* 2004, pp. 69–70). Not only is a 'global rush to commemorate' (Williams 2007) underway, but commemoration itself is becoming 'more global' (Gillis 1994, p. 14). It is 'beginning to escape the bounds of national political communities' as regional and global practices of memory are emerging (Bell 2006, p. 29). The national hold on memory, never entirely firm, has been loosened by international norms, narratives and finances. The most significant example of this has been the global spread of the memory of the Holocaust and of memory practices associated with it; and its role in defining new cosmopolitan 'sensibilities and moral-political obligations' (Levy and Sznaider 2002, p. 103). In the wake of this, national remembrance is employed not only to mould domestic legitimacy, but also to anchor ruling elites within international frameworks for legitimization (Hughes 2006b). Public remembrances are a focus for both domestic civic activity and associated contests over legitimacy (Olick and Robbins 1998, p. 126), and are also subject to international influences (Ashplant *et al.* 2004, p. 17). Memory has become 'transnationalized'.

The Rwanda case is shaped by and reflects the new dynamics of the politics of memory, but it has a particular character in that it is also framed by current international development cooperation practices. This article explores the intentions of international agencies and their impact on public remembrance, based on interviews, participant observation and documentary sources. Firstly, it outlines the historical relations between the international community and the state in Rwanda, before, during and after the 1994 genocide, as the context in which international contributions to memorials became possible. Then it explores the aims of donors and their role in the construction of genocide memorials, focusing on the creation of the most prominent national memorial museum, the Kigali Genocide Memorial Centre (KMC), in which international agencies took a leading part. Finally, it considers the effects of international intervention, examining the forms, narratives and practices of genocide remembrance it produced. It offers insight into the relations between the state and the international community in post-conflict reconstruction as well as the 'transnationalization' of public memory. International donors and NGOs collaborate with national elites in genocide memorialization and the project highlights their mutual interest in the symbolic constitution of political legitimacy.

International Interventions in Rwanda

International involvement in memory production in Rwanda takes place in a post-colonial state where external intervention has long been the norm. To understand the role of the international community and its relationship with the state in this task, we need to bear in mind a series of historical interactions. Firstly, the colonization of Rwanda from 1899–1962, in which initially German, then Belgian colonizers laid the structural foundations of the state; and marked out and politicized ethnic differences (Mamdani 2001). Secondly, the post-independence era in which Hutu elites became adept at garnering international support for development while pursuing discrimination and violence against Tutsis and fostering nationwide structural violence (Uvin 1998). Thirdly, the 1994 genocide in which Western governments were complicit (Melvern 2004).

The genocide exposed the limits of international concern for the lives of ordinary Rwandans. While from April–July 1994 up to a million people were killed by Hutu extremists aiming to eradicate Rwanda's minority Tutsi population (des Forges 1999, Prunier 1998), the major Western powers and the United Nations prevaricated. They treated the genocide as an episode in an ongoing war, launched by RPF rebels in October 1990, despite forewarning and knowledge of the systematic extermination as it occurred (Power 2002, Melvern 2004). Although a small contingent of international peacekeepers were on the ground to monitor a ceasefire in the war, they were given neither the means nor the mandate to act effectively (Dallaire 2004). Eventually, on 22 June the French launched a humanitarian mission, Opération Turquoise, but it came too late to save many lives and gave some leading perpetrators an escape route into exile, as was perhaps to be expected since France had supported the former regime of President Juvénal Habyarimana even as it prepared for genocide (Kroslak 2008).

It was not an international intervention, but an RPF victory over government forces in July 1994 which brought an end to the genocide. By then, heaps of corpses were decomposing in public buildings and on streets, or buried in shallow mass graves. Some two million citizens had fled into exile, and those that remained were divided by their experiences of violence. The country was in social and economic crisis (Prunier 1998). International support would be essential for recovery and Rwanda soon became the testing ground for an 'emerging post-conflict agenda' (Uvin 2001, p. 177).

Initially, donors held very different perspectives on the post-genocide regime, including on the extent to which they ought to take account of the legacy of the genocide in their assessments. Concerns about the lack of democracy under-pinned a reluctance to give aid directly (Uvin 2001, pp. 180–181). However, by 2003, Britain, the United States and the Netherlands were among the leading donors and Rwanda was receiving aid on a scale equivalent to 69 per cent of government spending (Zorbas 2007, p. 4). In 2005, the country was deemed a model reformer, gaining debt relief on the basis of its Poverty Reduction Strategy Programme.

Although the government of Rwanda followed international economic policy prescriptions, and gained substantial support, donors had less influence in the political sphere. Central to the Rwandese strategy for maintaining political autonomy was deploying the memory of the genocide, exploiting the guilt felt by development partners to fend off criticism. Rwanda 'managed to keep substantive donor "interventionism" at bay' (Zorbas 2007, p. 1), obtaining donor funding for justice and reconciliation initiatives strictly according to government parameters. It was in this context that certain donors decided to support memorialization as the tenth anniversary of the genocide approached in 2004, and in so doing, they gained a role in shaping the national narrative and reconstituting their own relations with Rwanda.

Aid for Genocide Remembrance

The burial and commemoration of the dead and the construction of memorials was a preoccupation of survivors immediately after the genocide, then became a concern of the state (Ibreck 2009, p. 67). By 2003, genocide memory was a prominent feature on Rwanda's landscape and in the national calendar. An official annual commemoration of the genocide was held from 7–13 April. Rwandans were called to memorial sites for reburials, to listen to government officials speak about the genocide and to hear survivors give testimony, in a national ritual of mourning. The remains of victims were still being reburied in dignity at memorial sites. Hundreds of memorials and burial sites had been established across the country. Six memorial sites were given the status of 'national sites' and selected for further development.

International support for memorialization was a response to government requests for aid in the development of national memorial museums and support for the commemoration of the tenth anniversary of the genocide. Donors therefore played a secondary role, in partnership with the state and survivors, and their involvement was relatively short term. Nevertheless, their contribu-tions were significant and enduring in the preservation and development of four memorials in particular: the Kigali Genocide Memorial Centre, the Murambi

Genocide Prevention Centre, the National Genocide Memorials at Ntarama and Nyarubuye and the Nyanza Genocide Memorial.

A handful of key donors provided the bulk of the funding for memorial sites: the UK Department for International Development (DFID), the government of the Netherlands, the William Jefferson Clinton Foundation, the government of Sweden and the Embassy of Belgium and, to a lesser extent, the German development agency, Deutsche Gesellschaft für Technische Zusammenarbeit (GTZ). The 2004 commemoration was sponsored by DFID, Belgium, the Netherlands and Germany, together with a wider group of donors, including Canada, the United Nations Development Programme (UNDP) and China (MIJESPOC 2004).

Aid was generally given for the remembrance of Rwandan genocide victims, with the exception of the memorial for the Belgian victims at Camp Kigali, a reminder that some members of the international community were directly affected. Funding was generally for improvements to existing memorials and was dispensed around the time of the tenth anniversary of the genocide, from 2003–4. By April 2004, MIJESPOC had raised some US$7 million for memorialization from donor countries (Hirondelle 2004). It went mainly to the Rwandan ministry responsible for genocide memory, the Ministry of Youth, Sports and Culture (MIJESPOC), and to a UK-based NGO, Aegis Trust, which the ministry authorized to design and implement projects at the Murambi Genocide Prevention Centre and the KMC.

International involvement in the construction of memorials varied with each project. For the 2004 commemoration, MIJESPOC established an organizing body which brought together representatives of the government, the national survivors' association and international donors who had contributed funds; it also appointed Aegis Trust's director to a decision-making role on the steering committee. At the Murambi Genocide Prevention Centre, Aegis Trust, the Rwandan National Museum, the local government and MIJESPOC forged a partnership in 2003, raising a total of €350,000 for improvements to the site (Aegis Trust 2004b). At KMC there was a similar arrangement with Aegis raising US$2 million to develop the site from donors working with Kigali's mayor, who had established and built the memorial site in 2000. At the Ntarama and Nyarubuye sites DFID committed £695,000 to protect the former churches (Butera 2006) and hired British architects and a Kenyan construction company to carry out improvements based on a proposal by the Minister of Youth, Culture and Sport in 2003. On a smaller scale, the Belgian government contributed funds to the ministry to create a memorial garden and a sculpture at Nyanza-Kicukiro in Kigali.

The Aims

The rationale for giving aid to memorialization was to promote reconciliation within Rwanda and to contribute to genocide prevention both nationally and internationally, as representatives of the principal donors explained. The memorials were associated with a post-conflict programme to rebuild the state in Rwanda, in alliance with the government. It was anticipated that they could contribute to reconciliation and ultimately to good governance: 'DFID is interested in peace and reconciliation as a prerequisite for development. The overarching aim is poverty reduction . . . supporting the memory of the genocide is part of supporting good governance' (C. Kirk, personal communication, 2 August 2006). Memorials were a possible means to encourage Rwandans to develop a shared understanding of the past and to learn its lessons: 'knowing your own history is probably going to help to avoid it happening again. It is a tool to understand better and a tool for reconciliation' (S. Decartier, personal communication, 21 August 2006). These personal views are consonant with the idea that memory can help to heal communities, rebuilding societies (Hamber 2004, p. 1). International donors place emphasis on the 'history and memory of the 1994 genocide' as part of a wider push for democracy, reconciliation and healing (Webley 2004, p. 124).

International actors also linked memory preservation and education to the international obligation to combat genocide. They invoked the post-Holocaust injunction 'never again', on the assumption that 'those who don't remember the past are condemned to repeat it' (C. Kirk, personal communication, 2 August 2006). They spoke of the rights of victims to recognition and justice. According to a representative of the Netherlands, 'The tragedy of what happened should be made known, that's clear . . . there is a legitimate right for victims to have no ambiguity about what happened' (personal communication, 7 August 2006).

However, even those donors who gave most support to memorialization worried that memorials could exacerbate tensions in the sensitive environment of post-genocide Rwanda. They noted that public memory is selective; that some Rwandans do not welcome the genocide memorialization and that some seek recognition for other victims of human rights abuses, including RPF war crimes. Off the record, one donor representative commented on disputes over the past among Rwandans and of the view of some that only part of the history of the atrocities has been acknowledged publicly: 'there is a perception of one sidedness which can become a rallying point internationally . . . it is a sensitive issue' (personal communication, August 2006). Another called attention to suppressed memories, the silences about RPF war crimes and the tensions surrounding them (personal communication, August 2006). A third suggested that burial of the bones which lie exposed at memorial sites might be necessary 'to turn the page' and pointed out that 'the suffering of Hutu women exposed to violence is not remembered . . . there are forgotten people in this region' (personal communication, August 2006). Moreover, as one embassy representative pointed out, the social impact of memory projects will be complex and long term: 'the benefits are not so clear. They're visible in one or two generations, at the moment you cannot measure the results' (personal communication, August 2006). These comments reveal a wariness of the role of the Rwandan state in memorialization, and a desire to mitigate political exploitation of genocide remembrance: 'There is a danger that they could become focal points of accusation ... tools for propagating collective guilt ... it is up to those responsible for the memorials to see that they are used to educate for a better future, to foster understanding, to make them inclusive' (personal communication, March 2005). International donors sought to mould rather than to endorse state-led memorialization.

Donors were also intent upon shaping relationships with Rwanda in a broader sense. Funding memorialization was a means to express regret for the failure of the international community to halt the genocide in 1994. Contributions to memorials, and participation in commemoration internationally, came in the wake of revelations about the conduct of the international community in 1994 (United Nations 1999) which called into question the moral character of world leaders and the notion of 'an international community'. They were a response to the sustained critique by Rwandan leaders of Western powers and their use of annual commemorations to demand displays of 'repentance' (Loir 2005, p. 416). Loir describes Rwanda's leading development donors, including the US, UK, the Netherlands, Sweden and Belgium as 'literally paralysed by the postponed guilt' for a 'genocide that could have been prevented' (2005, p. 419). Steele argues that international support for commemoration arose from guilt and a wish to demonstrate solidarity (2006 p. 11). This was confirmed by the DFID representative who observed that the UK 'shares collective guilt', having 'failed to deliver' on its international responsibility to intervene in 1994 and that memorials were a means to 'show solidarity with Rwanda' (C. Kirk, personal communication, 2 August 2006).

Representatives of governments and institutions evidently saw their contributions to memorials as a means of expressing their genuine regret. Yet alongside this moral imperative they understood its relevance to foreign policy concerns, including repairing their own image and that of the international community, and cementing their relationship with the Rwandan state. Expressions of sorrow have political currency. As a Belgian official explained, the memorials are part of forging good diplomatic relationships with the government of Rwanda (S. Decartier, personal communication, 21 August 2006). Aiding memorialization offered a way to strengthen ties with Rwanda, including by shaping its national memory.

Making Memory at the Kigali Genocide Memorial Centre

Foreign donors have contributed to the construction of public memory in Rwanda both by giving funds to projects proposed by the state, and by employing foreign NGOs and consultants to carry out important aspects of the implementation. Their involvement has varied, as have their relations with Rwandan officials and civil society. There have been local challenges to such interventions, with tensions and disputes between national and international actors in projects in Murambi and Nyanza-Kicukiro (Ibreck 2009, pp. 172–179, 113, Laville 2006). Nevertheless, the impact of international engagement has been visible and substantial at the principal national memorial in the capital, the KMC.

The KMC is the only purpose-built museum of the genocide, situated in the capital, and the burial place for an estimated 250,000 genocide victims from surrounding areas. It opened in April 2004 and has since been visited by droves of Rwandans as well as international dignitaries and tourists. Fifteen hundred survivors visited each day during the first week, while in the first three months of its opening around 60,000 people came, over 7,000 of them 'from the International Community' (KMC n.d.). Like other genocide memorials in Rwanda, it hosts official ceremonies during national commemorations and displays the remains of victims and relics of the slaughter, but unlike most it also includes an exhibition of the history of the genocide in narrative form with survivor testimony and photographs. By virtue of its location and status, the KMC is an important example which can shed light on whether and how international involvement has altered the aims, processes and forms of memorials in Rwanda.

Genocide Education and Mourning

The KMC aims to fulfil two main purposes: to educate Rwandans and visitors from outside the country about the genocide; and to serve as a place of mourning for survivors and relatives of the dead. Its educational function is incorporated into the structure and the everyday activities of the centre. There are permanent exhibitions on the genocide in Rwanda and on comparative genocides, a documentation centre, a schools programme, a conference facility and a website. According to Aegis Trust, the UK-based NGO specializing in Holocaust memorialization which took on the development of the site, the aim is to reach out to Rwandans, but at the same time to draw in and inform visitors to the country: to 'engage and challenge an international visitor base' (KMC n.d.). The other priority is to give 'acknowledgement' to the victims in order to: 'help survivors with healing' (J. Smith, personal communication, 20 January 2005); the centre contains a cemetery, a memorial garden and an exhibition dedicated to child victims.

The instructive aims of the centre fit with the aspirations of donors to contribute to reconciliation and genocide prevention, while the concern for survivors accords with their desire to express regret. This is not to say that donor concerns predominated, since the state seeks to promote similar aims through memorialization (Ibreck 2009, p. 73) and survivors have struggled independently to create sites of mourning (Ibreck 2010). However, international actors had a key role in the process of memory construction, determining the ways in which aims were translated into narratives, forms and practices.

A Transnational Process

Before the involvement of international agencies, the KMC was a burial ground, with an empty building and a tentative plan for development. Kigali City Council had designated this site in Gisozi, close to the centre of the city, as a cemetery for the corpses of genocide victims unearthed around the city. The mayor, Theoneste Mutsindashyaka, organized the construction of a building there in 2000 and it was originally used to display some of the victims' remains. According to the director of Aegis Trust, the intention was to expand this use of the site as a charnel house, by creating 'three big bays filled with shelves of skulls and bones...they wanted to run sounds of babies screaming and the killings going on'. The mayor sought the support of international donors to sponsor the development of the memorial early on, but received a negative response. After a visit to the Beth Shalom Holocaust Centre in Nottingham, England, he met with and formed a partnership with its directors, the founders of Aegis Trust (J. Smith, personal communication, 20 January 2005).

The plan for the KMC chimed with an initiative by a group of political and civil society leaders in Rwanda who had formed a committee to organise a new memorial in Kigali for the 2004 anniversary. They wanted a memorial comparable to Holocaust memorials in Europe and the US. They planned to raise US$10 million and did not intend to use the Gisozi site, viewing it as 'too small'. Aegis Trust's director met with the group and encouraged them to scale down their ambitions. 'I said it's a lot of money, there are people with HIV/AIDS, survivors with nothing. Rwanda is a developing country, then maybe in another ten years time...'. Their response was to ask him to come up with a proposal for Gisozi. Aegis Trust developed the plan and, in partnership with Kigali City Council, it persuaded donors to contribute to the development of the site (J. Smith, personal communication, 20 January 2005).

Aegis Trust took just four months to create a memorial garden and the three permanent exhibitions and the project was completed in time to host the commemoration of the tenth anniversary of the genocide in April 2004 (Smith 2006). As the centrepiece of the exhibition, it produced a series of panels based on images of the genocide, with text written by Aegis Trust directors; these were all produced outside Rwanda: 'designed in the UK at the Aegis Trust head office by their design team, and shipped to Rwanda to be installed' (KMC n.d.) for the official opening. Although the organization employed 100 local staff, it relied on staff in the UK throughout the production process, and as the work progressed and the deadline approached, 15 of them were brought to Rwanda, 'flown in for various expert roles' (KMC n.d.).

Aegis Trust's plan for the site was 'modelled on' their own experience at the Beth Shalom Holocaust Centre in Nottingham (KMC n.d.); Rwandan officials had minimal input into the content or design of the process. As Aegis's director explained: 'They left us to do the exhibition...They didn't appreciate at all the impact potentially a memorial centre in Kigali could have.' The main stipulation made by Minister Ngarambe, responsible for memorials at the time, was that the

KMC should condemn the 'ideology of genocide' and not generalize about the perpetrators, or appear to place the blame on Hutus (J. Smith, personal communication, 20 January 2005). Some changes were suggested by President Paul Kagame during a preview three days before the opening, but these were minor additions. He recommended that some documentary sources to illustrate the history of racial ideology in Rwanda could be added, and asked that the exhibition, which refers to the 'role of the Belgians' in the history of the genocide, should also acknowledge the apology they issued in 2000 (J. Smith, personal communication, 20 January 2005).

The process of designing the KMC was led by Aegis Trust; it consulted with the government and survivors, but at the opening of the memorial it declared with some justification that it was 'shaping the memory of Rwanda's genocide' (Aegis Trust 2004a). After 2004, the organization continued to manage the project, with a board of Rwandans, including an MP, a member of the city council, a representative of Ibuka and a member of the National Unity and Reconciliation Commission (NURC). They raised funds for its ongoing costs from Rwandan businesses as well as continuing to appeal to international donors for support (J. Smith, personal communication, January 2005).

The KMC is an example of transnational memory-making: though it originated with national elites, the idea was inspired by international Holocaust memorials, adding weight to the observation that in contemporary times state discourse on the past is generated 'from interaction within transnational arenas' (Ashplant *et al*. 2004, p. 53). Moreover, because of a lack of funds and capacity to produce similar within Rwanda, a foreign NGO supported by international donors took up the reins.

The New Genocide Memorial Museum

The character of the memory-making process is echoed in the form of the KMC. The cream villa-style building overlooks the surrounding area of Gisozi, Kigali, from a gated and guarded hilltop. In terms of content and presentation it invites comparison with some Holocaust memorial museums (Steele 2006, p. 7). The building is surrounded by a rose garden cemetery, and a wall with the names of victims engraved upon it runs alongside the mass graves. The naming of the dead is used to individualize victims through displays of photographs and belongings, in a personalization of history reminiscent of Holocaust memorials which seek to 'rehumanize' the victims (Young 1993, pp. 337–342). In this vein, among the most moving elements of the museum are a modest, almost haphazard, display of photographs of genocide victims, mostly donated by their surviving relatives, and the 'children's memorial', where images of young victims are displayed with details of their names, ages, likes and dislikes.

The museum evokes sympathy for victims but is also designed to testify to the horror of the genocide. Evidence of the genocide is on display in 'physical remnants', human remains, clothing and belongings of victims. These elements are often used to create authenticity (Williams 2007); they communicate the enormity of the losses, leaving a profound sense of disturbance, previously observed in Holocaust memorials (Edkins 2003, p. 152). Bloodstained clothing at KMC conveys the atrocities in an 'international language of suffering' (Davis 2009, p. 144). Aegis Trust has sought to convey this too in its display of human remains—the memorial retains some of the bones of the dead which had been central to the plan envisaged by Rwandan leaders for the site; however, these are covered over by dark glass, to suggest the care and respect associated with burials, offering a 'compromise' which contrasts with their raw and shocking presentation at other memorials in Rwanda (Williams 2007, p. 42).

These and other aspects of the KMC, including the exhibitions, the visitor book, artworks, video screens showing survivor testimony, air conditioning and glossy brochures conform to the expectations of international visitors (Steele 2006, p. 9). As Shannon Davis writes, the museum is structured around visual 'cues' with which international tourists can connect (Davis 2009).

Whether or not the KMC had been funded by donors, we would expect to see some resemblances to museums elsewhere, and an attempt to appeal internationally. Paul Williams treats memorial museums as a 'global institutional development' (2007, p. 9), finding a set of conventions in their choices about which objects and images to display and how. In a period where experts in Holocaust memorialization or transitional justice interact, and where post-conflict countries see the possibilities for 'dark tourism' to contribute to development, we can perceive transnational practices of memorialization and the fusion of local imperatives and imaginaries with international norms. The question of what a memorial should look like and contain is resolved in 'global entanglements...the interweaving of diverse transnational memories, knowledge formations and logics of representation' (Schwenkel 2006, p. 5). This interweaving applies even where state officials and private entrepreneurs generate memorials (Schwenkel 2006, p. 5), but the external influence on the style and content of the exhibitions is striking at KMC, based on Aegis Trust's formative UK Holocaust memorial, Beth Shalom.

The Symbolic Reconstruction of Rwanda

Given that KMC is the product of a transnational process, its account of the genocide cannot be said to be determined by the present political interests of national elites in the direct way that memorials often are (Misztal 2003, p. 56). Nevertheless, like other memorials it is designed to encourage both memory and forgetting; it is implicated in masking elements of the past likely to undermine the present social order (Edkins 2003, p. 229) and forging a shared understanding of the past necessary for the constitution of 'an imagined political community' (Anderson 1991, p. 6). To uncover how the past is represented at memorial sites—the meanings and the notions of identity generated, and the power relations underpinning them—we can draw on the technique of discourse analysis, looking at which people, institutions or practices are validated and which are marginalized or viewed negatively (Hughes 2006a, p. 63). The obvious focus for analysis at the KMC are the two permanent exhibitions—the first narrates the history of the genocide in Rwanda in three sections, and the second 'wasted lives' exhibition examines genocides around the world. Both exhibitions include photographs and text produced on colour panels in the three official languages of Rwanda (Kinyarwanda, English and French); together, they convey an image of Rwanda and its relationship to the international community.

The Nation

From the first panel, the exhibition on the 1994 genocide promotes a vision of national unity. It narrates history in the first person plural, as if composed by a collective of Rwandans, sharing a consensus about the past: 'This has been our home for centuries. We are one people. We speak one language. We have one history...This is about our past and our future' (Kigali Memorial Centre 2004, p. 8). The account links the genocide to colonial roots and to the ideology of Hutu power. It depicts a pre-colonial harmony in which Hutus and Tutsis 'had lived in peace for many centuries' (Kigali Memorial Centre 2004, p. 9) and explains that the politicization of identity was the result of bureaucratic interventions of the European colonists, followed by the manipulation of post-independence elites pursuing 'fascist' policies of ethnic cleansing of and discrimination against Tutsis (Kigali Memorial Centre 2004, p. 11). It notes the massive internal displacement of Rwandans as a result of the war launched by the RPF in 1990, but indicates that the war was in pursuit of 'equal rights and the rule of law' (Kigali Memorial Centre 2004, p. 12).

The emphasis is consistently upon the intentional and sustained nature of the violence and its status as a genocide, asserting: 'it was genocide from the first day...no Tutsi was exempt' (Kigali Memorial Centre 2004, p. 20). We learn that the killers principally targeted Tutsis, along with Hutu political opponents and those who refused to participate. We are told of the 'evil' of the perpetrators (Kigali Memorial Centre 2004, p. 22) and the courage of the resisters—a section is devoted to Hutu 'heroes', who hid their neighbours or friends at grave personal risk. The horror of the slaughter is conveyed, in part by converting statistics into individuals: 'the genocidaires did not kill a million people. They killed one, then another, then another' (Kigali Memorial Centre 2004, p. 22).

The narrative successfully contradicts some of the myths and stereotypes of Tutsis which informed the perpetrators of the genocide, but it omits significant aspects of the context. For instance, neither the assassination in 1993 of Melchior Ndadaye, the first democratically elected Hutu President of Burundi, nor RPF killings during the 1990–94 war are highlighted, yet both are central to understanding the mindset of the killers (Straus 2006). Omissions are inevitable; an exhibition cannot capture all the complexities of the process which led to genocide. However, what is remarkable about this account is that it is presented as an accepted truth about the past, apparently in the interests of national unity. First Rwanda is described as divided into a 'nation of brutal, sadistic merciless killers and of innocent victims, overnight' (Kigali Memorial Centre 2004, p. 21); then the entire nation is seen to be suffering together: 'Rwanda was dead' (Kigali Memorial Centre 2004, p. 22). As Williams notes, the aim of promoting reconciliation is apparent in the presentation of the violence in neutral terms and in an effort to avoid apportioning blame, representing the atrocity as a consequence of 'general human failure'. It describes those responsible as 'genocidaires' and the victims as 'the nation' (2007, p. 135). The exhibition concludes that 'we remember the victims of the past' (Kigali Memorial Centre 2004, p. 40), placing the genocide and its consequences at a distance and envisaging a present in which all Rwandans are in accord, and remember together.

In this view, the conflict is over and the country is deemed to be on the right path: 'Rwanda is determined to work toward reconciliation' (Kigali Memorial Centre 2004, p. 41). The narrative concludes with an agenda for progress and a justification of the memorial's existence, claiming that the education of Rwandans about the genocide will promote understanding and reflection 'on values and actions' (Kigali Memorial Centre 2004, p. 41). The memorial promises to change popular attitudes and repair trust, and endorses the existing strategies for post-conflict reconstruction being pursued by the government of Rwanda, with aid from international donors.

Aegis Trust's director acknowledges that the KMC promotes a selective memory, but argues that its contribution is to encourage an ongoing process of engagement with the past:

> It's true that we are depicting only part of what happened in Rwanda. We are influencing national identity in a way not reflective of real history but you can't do everything. What we are aiming to do is to foster an environment in which people can talk about their experiences...The narrative about the past does change and will change in Rwanda. But it is where it is and we will work with it. (Smith personal communication, 20 January 2005)

Since the completion of the exhibition, important elements of the narrative have changed: Aegis Trust originally avoided references to ethnicity in line with the official approach, but recently the government took the decision to amend all its references to the '1994 Genocide' to the 'Genocide against the Tutsis'— the KMC has yet to follow suit. Meanwhile, the enduring public silence about Hutu suffering threatens to undermine the hope that the KMC can promote greater openness about the past. Lemarchand condemns the 'spuriously unifying official memory' promoted by the RPF regime, which is echoed in aspects of the KMC narrative, as exclusive, obliterating elements of the past and obstructing the potential for interethnic dialogue and reconciliation (2009, pp. 99–100).

Fundamentally, the KMC account of the genocide resonates with a perspective on history promoted by the RPF, conjuring up an image of pre-colonial harmony

An International Community

The exhibition on the history of the genocide is highly critical of the international response to the genocide in 1994. Firstly, we learn of the failure to intervene to halt the killings. A copy of the 'genocide fax' is displayed, to show that the UN was made aware of an alleged plan to exterminate Tutsis in January 1994, but was reluctant to act: 'The world withdrew...and watched as a million people were slaughtered' (Kigali Memorial Centre 2004, p. 28). French support for the Habyarimana regime, including the financing of an arms deal and the training of government troops, is noted, and the French military intervention, Opération Turquoise, is criticized for 'providing a safe zone for genocidaires' (Kigali Memorial Centre 2004, p. 29).

Although the conduct of the international community in 1994 is explicitly condemned, the exhibition encourages faith in the idea of an international community and its promise of humanitarianism. Apart from the criticism of the French, the narrative focuses mainly on sins of omission: the failure to intervene. There is no mention, for instance, of the negative impact of IMF/World Bank structural adjustment policies (Storey 2001) or of the role of past development policies in contributing to 'structural violence' and the conditions for genocide (Uvin 1998). Moreover, we are reminded that not all colonial interventions were negative: 'schooling and medicine developed, as did the infrastructure. Useful export markets...opened up' (Kigali Memorial Centre 2004, p. 9). We learn that external intervention was the best means through which the genocide might have been halted: 'as few as 5,000 troops with authority to enforce peace could stop the genocide' (Kigali Memorial Centre 2004, p. 26). We find out that staff at the UN soon realized their error (Kigali Memorial Centre 2004, p. 26) and that, from the outset, international human rights workers were not 'fooled' by the Habyarimana regime (Kigali Memorial Centre 2004, p. 14).

The KMC presents a liberal humanitarian perspective on the problem of genocide and on the possible solutions. As Steele comments, it: '[E]mbodies and serves present international criminal law and dominant human rights discourse...the memorial directly mirrors, and in turn extends, the *Convention on the Prevention and Punishment of Genocide*' (2006, p. 7). The focus of human rights discourse on the individual as the bearer of rights is evident in the efforts to break down the mass of genocide victims into named individuals, killed 'one after another' (Kigali Memorial Centre 2004, p. 22); each had a universal right to protection from genocide. Universalism is also apparent in the 'wasted lives' exhibition, with its comparative analysis of the tragic events of genocides in Namibia, Armenia, Germany, Cambodia and the Balkans. Genocide is shown to be an international problem, and the exhibition makes clear that the international community has a responsibility to respond, both in terms of prevention and protection. The implication is that international humanitarian intervention is the answer, consistent with the 'Responsibility to Protect' approach. As Aegis Trust's director Stephen Smith explains: 'Memorials are also important for the international community and for policy makers to reflect on our past failures to prevent genocide, and about our responsibility to protect those who remain under threat, both now and in the future' (cited in Davis 2009, p. 164).

Responses

By concentrating on the narratives at KMC we inevitably simplify and marginalize other aspects of the memorial. Meaning is made, in part, through the juxtaposition of narratives, symbols and artefacts—for instance the site also contains traces of the past, including the human remains, clothing and photographs of the victims; such displays evoke the trauma of genocide and challenge political attempts to make sense of it (Edkins 2003). Although narrative reconstructions of events are brought together with fragments of the past and individual recollections and 'assigned common meaning', this meaning is not fixed, but may be rearranged and or reworked as visitors interact with memorials (Young 1993, p. xii). To gauge the effects of the KMC we ought to also take account of the uses of and responses to the site.

At the time of writing, the KMC has only been open for seven years, but has received many visitors from various backgrounds. First and foremost, Rwanda's genocide survivors have embraced the opportunity to come and remember or rebury their loved ones. They have contributed testimony and photographs to the exhibitions and some have worked there, including as guides or researchers. Relatives of the dead have come to bury the victims of the genocide in dignity, to honour them and to mourn their loss.

Other Rwandans visit less frequently but, as one member of staff commented, 'people are finally realising it concerns all Rwandans' (KMC employee, personal communication, July 2006). The centre is used for official ceremonies and hosts large crowds during the annual commemoration. It is also used for genocide education: Rwandan officials visit the centre and staff from government ministries or local government are brought there to learn about the genocide. On 19 June 2008, the centre launched a genocide education programme, bringing together several thousand youths and elders to learn from Rwanda's past (Aegis Trust 2008). Schools, public institutions and even private companies have begun to participate, booking their staff on visits.

The Rwandan Prime Minister, Bernard Makuza, wrote in the KMC visitors' book: 'You are the stone on which we will build a Rwanda without conflict' (Smith

2006). However, as yet we know little of the views of Rwandans who visit the centre, or of attitudes towards it among those who do not. People's attitudes towards reconciliation and commemoration policies vary: Rwanda 'presents an interesting case study of the limits of a government's ability to shape the collective memory of a population' (Longman and Rutagengwa 2006, p. 243). Genocide denial, political extremism and suppressed memories simmer beneath the surface (Lemarchand 2009), and may threaten the relative peace established after the genocide. On rare occasions these issues have come to light at the KMC. The most extreme negative response was a grenade attack upon the centre during the annual week of commemoration in April 2008, in which one of the guards was killed (Aegis Rwanda 2008b). The attack was an isolated act of violence, but more significantly opposition presidential candidate Victoire Ingabire recently issued a strong critique at the KMC, which is likely to have wider support. She chose to make her first speech there upon her return to Rwanda in January 2010, stating: 'Reconciliation has a long way to go . . . Looking at this memorial, it only stops at the genocide committed to Tutsis; there is still another role that concerns the massacres committed to Hutus. Their relatives are asking themselves: "When will our concerns be discussed"?' (BBC News 2010a).

Despite these tensions, for the most part, the centre is tranquil and attracts a healthy number of visitors. More people visit the KMC than any other memorial site in Rwanda, many recording positive views in the visitor book. In 2006 it is estimated that over 150,000 people visited the centre (Smith 2006); at the time of my visit in July 2006, the centre had just hosted some 500 schoolchildren on an educational visit. The KMC is promoting 'social practices of visitation', which, as Williams explains, build on existing remembrance rituals, but take time to establish (2007, p. 5). This applies both among Rwandans and among tourists and foreign visitors, for whom a tour of the site is generally on the itinerary. Its success among tourists suggests that, like memorial sites elsewhere, the KMC has become an international commodity in a 'transnational economy of memory' (Schwenkel 2006, p. 5).

Meanwhile, for politicians and diplomats visiting Rwanda a visit to KMC may serve as a personal expression of regret, a ritual of initiation into Rwanda's political society, or a symbolic act to be used politically—former US President George W. Bush, for instance, praised the exhibition for reminding us 'there is evil in the world and evil must be confronted' (Aegis Rwanda 2008a), reiterating his discourse on the war on terror. Overall, the KMC has become part of how the international community engages with Rwanda and of the image Rwanda presents to the world.

Imagining Post-Genocide Rwanda

The narrative at KMC condemns the extreme nationalism expressed in the genocide, but it endorses the nation-building project of the current Rwandan government in its narratives and practices. It imagines a present-day Rwanda at peace and supported by a moral international community which has recognized its failings and strengthened its commitment to combat genocide. The construction of a memorial itself signals that the violence has ended. This is reinforced by its message of 'never again', an idea which here, as elsewhere, directs us to the past and to the future without recognition of the pervasiveness of atrocities in the present (Verbeek 2007, p. 223). While the memorial was being built, Rwanda was at war in the neighbouring Democratic Republic of Congo, a conflict linked to the 1994 genocide—in which Rwandan forces have committed human rights abuses (Prunier 2009) and are suspected of genocide (BBC News 2010b), and a crisis to which the international community failed to mount an effective response.

Donor support for genocide memorialization in Rwanda reflects the ambitions and approaches of international policy-makers in post-conflict arenas where strengthening the interior sovereignty of the state is perceived as a means to promote peace (Humphrey 2005, p. 207). In particular, reconciliation projects are 'designed to promote individual well-being and healing through behavioural and attitudinal change as the basis for conflict prevention' (Humphrey 2005, p. 205). Such interventions intend not just to restore order but to realize social and political transformation to conform to liberal norms (Duffield 2001, p. 258). They are underpinned by a conception of sovereignty as 'conditional' and of peace-building as reconstructing states and influencing populations directly. They promote 'a particular kind of globalisation' which reinforces the state while cultivating particular norms of 'what a state should look like and how it should act' (Paris 2002, p. 654) and extending the reach and role of international actors within it.

Conclusion

International support for genocide memorials in Rwanda has three main aims. Firstly, sponsors aim to promote reconciliation among Rwandans by changing Rwandans' attitudes to the past and cultivating an idea of a unified nation. They see a memorial as a mechanism for contributing to this. Secondly, they intend to promote the cause of genocide prevention worldwide on the premise that international cooperation and commitment is necessary to combat genocide. This is based upon faith in the idea that 'never again' depends on remembering and learning lessons from past atrocities. Thirdly, international actors engage in memorialization as an act of solidarity and diplomacy to express regret for the losses of the genocide. This serves to build personal or institutional credibility and to support international norms.

As a result, international donors have become involved in a project of imagining a new political community in Rwanda. This is a hybrid domestic-international project. The example of the KMC indicates a partnership between the state and the international community in the symbolic reconstruction of the nation. It is not clear that this project will have the desired impact; memories in Rwanda are seared by the divisions and trauma of the genocide and other past conflicts (Ibreck 2009) and public memory is everywhere a focus for contestation (Misztal 2003, p. 73). But it shows how Rwandan elites are influenced by transnational discourses and how they seek external support for post-conflict reconstruction and to construct their political legitimacy, an established practice in this donor-dependent state. It also reveals how international actors seek to repair Rwanda as a nation, by fostering the legitimacy of its current rulers while drawing it further under the wing of the international community.

International interventions in the memorialization of the 1994 genocide resonate with what we know about the state-sponsored politics of memory at a national level. Like the state itself, international agencies respond to challenges posed to their legitimacy by a traumatic event in which they were implicated. Like national elites, they produce an idea of the nation through commemoration, and they use memorials to assert their difference from those responsible for past atrocities and to construct moral legitimacy (see Connerton 1989, p. 7). National and international practices of memory have become fused, as each seeks legitimacy from the other. Rwandans today are taught their national memory through an international prism, while global norms of preventing and punishing genocide are tied to a particular Rwandan political project, which relies heavily on symbolic remembrance. This fusion is also directly related to contemporary modes and strategies of international peace-building which seek to transform people and government in post-conflict arenas to fit a liberal international order—an endeavour which relies on promoting the notion of a moral international community. As such, international contributions to public remembrance in post-genocide Rwanda have as much to do with the reconstruction of an 'international community' as with the healing of a broken society.

Acknowledgements

The author is very grateful to all the individuals who generously gave their time to participate in research in Rwanda, which was the basis for this article, and all those who helped to facilitate and support this research, carried out with ESRC 1+3 PhD studentship funding. She also thanks two anonymous reviewers for their valuable suggestions and Vanessa Pupavac for comments on a related piece of work.

References

Aegis Rwanda, 2008a. Bush visit to Rwanda genocide memorial, 19 Feb. Available from: http://www.aegistrust.org/Aegis-Rwanda/bush-visit-to-rwanda-genocide-memorial-troubling-parallels-between-past-and-present.html [Accessed 10 June 2010].

Aegis Rwanda, 2008b.Terrorist attack on Rwandan genocide memorial, 11 Apr. Available from: http://www.aegistrust.org/Aegis-Rwanda/terrorist-attack-on-rwandan-genocide-memorial-increases-aegis-determination-to-tell-the-story.html [Accessed 10 June 2010].

Aegis Trust, 2004a. 10 years on: shaping the memory of Rwanda's genocide. Press Release, 7 Apr. Kigali: Aegis Trust.

Aegis Trust, 2004b. Progress of the project at Murambi. Unpublished progress report. Kigali: Aegis Trust.

Aegis Trust, 2008. Aegis launches genocide education programme in Rwanda, 19 Jun. Available from: http://www.aegistrust.org/index.php?option=com_content&task=view&id=757&Itemid=88 [Accessed 25 March 2009].

Anderson, B., 1991. *Imagined communities: reflections on the origin and spread of nationalism*. Revised ed. London/New York: Verso.

Ashplant, T.G., Dawson, G. and Roper, M., 2004. The politics of war memory and commemoration: contexts, structures and dynamics. *In*: T.G. Ashplant, G. Dawson and M. Roper, eds. *Commemorating war, the politics of memory*. New Jersey: Transaction Publishers, 3–85

BBC News, 2010a. Rwanda politician prompts row over genocide memorial, 18 Jan. Available from: http://news.bbc.co.uk/1/hi/world/africa/8466780.stm [Accessed 15 June 2010].

BBC News, 2010b. UN report says DR Congo killings 'may be genocide', 1 Oct. Available from: http://www.bbc.co.uk/news/world-africa-11450093 [Accessed 2 November 2010].

Bell, D., 2006. Introduction. *In*: D. Bell, ed. *Memory, trauma, and world politics: reflections on the relationship between past and present*. Basingstoke: Palgrave Macmillan, 1–29.

Butera, N., 2006. Update on Rwanda 10. DFID internal memo, 27 Jul. Kigali: DfID.

Connerton, P., 1989. *How societies remember*. Cambridge: Cambridge University Press.

Dallaire, R., Lt.Gen., 2004. *Shake hands with the devil: the failure of humanity in Rwanda*. London: Arrow Books Ltd.

Davis, E., 2005. *Memories of state: politics, history and collective identity in modern Iraq*. Berkeley/Los Angeles: University of California Press.

Davis, S., 2009. *The marking of memory and the right to remember*. Thesis (PhD). Lincoln University.

des Forges, A., 1999. *Leave none to tell the story*. Available from: http://www.hrw.org/reports/1999/rwanda/ [Accessed 10 July 2007].

Duffield, M., 2001. *Global governance and the new wars: the merging of development and security*. London: Zed Books.

Edkins, J., 2003. *Trauma and the memory of politics*. Cambridge: Cambridge University Press.

Gillis, J.R., 1994. Memory and identity: the history of a relationship. *In*: J.R. Gillis, ed. *Commemorations, the politics of national identity*. Princeton, NJ: Princeton University Press, 3–24.

Hamber, B., 2004. Public memorials and reconciliation processes in Northern Ireland. Paper presented at the 'Trauma and Transitional Justice in Divided Societies Conference', Airlie House, Warrington, Virginia, USA, 27–29 Mar.

Hirondelle, 2004. Seven heads of state to attend genocide commemoration, 2 Apr.

Hughes, R., 2006a. *Fielding genocide: post-1979 Cambodia and the geopolitics of memory*. Thesis (PhD). The University of Melbourne.

Hughes, R., 2006b. Nationalism and memory at the Tuol Sleng Museum of Genocide Crimes, Phnom Penh, Cambodia. *In*: K. Hodgkin and S. Radstone, eds. *Memory, history, nation, contested pasts.* New Brunswick, NJ: Transaction Publishers, 175–192.

Humphrey, M., 2005. Reconciliation and the therapeutic state. *Journal of international studies*, 26 (3), 203–220.

Ibreck, R., 2009. *Remembering humanity: the politics of genocide memorialisation in Rwanda.* Thesis (PhD). University of Bristol.

Ibreck, R., 2010. The politics of mourning: survivor contributions to memorials in post-genocide Rwanda. *Memory studies*, 3 (4), 330–343.

Kigali Memorial Centre, 2004. *Jenocide*. Kigali: Aegis Trust.

KMC, n.d., The Kigali Genocide Memorial Centre. Available from: http://www.kigalimemorialcentre.org/old/index-2.html] [Accessed 2 July 2008].

Kroslak, D., 2008. *The French betrayal of Rwanda.* Bloomington: Indiana University Press.

Laville, S., 2006. Two years late and mired in controversy: the British memorial to Rwanda's past, UK charity's plans for massacre site criticised. Centre is 'monotonous', say prominent Rwandans. *The Guardian*, 13 Nov. Available from: http://www.guardian.co.uk [Accessed on 28 September 2009].

Lemarchand, R., 2009. *The dynamics of violence in Central Africa.* Philadelphia: University of Pennsylvania Press.

Levy, D. and Sznaider, N., 2006. *The holocaust and memory in the global age.* Philadelphia, PA: Temple University Press.

Loir, G., 2005. Rwanda le régime de la dette perpétuelle' De l'instrumentalisation des massacres et du génocide en relations internationales. *Outre-Terre*, 11 (2), 415–421.

Longman, T. and Rutagengwa, T., 2006. Memory and violence in postgenocide Rwanda. *In*: E.G. Bay and D.L. Donham, eds. *States of violence, politics, youth, and memory in contemporary Africa.* Charlottesville/London: University of Virginia Press, 236–260.

Mamdani, M., 2001. *When victims become killers, colonialism, nativism, and the genocide in Rwanda.* Oxford: James Currey.

Melvern, L., 2004. *Conspiracy to murder: the Rwandan genocide.* New York: Verso.

MIJESPOC, 2004. Final report on the International Conference on Genocide, Intercontinental Hotel, Kigali, 4–6 Apr.

Misztal, B.A., 2003. *Theories of social remembering.* Maidenhead: Open University Press.

Olick, J.K. and Robbins, J., 1998. Social memory studies: from 'collective memory' to the historical sociology of mnemonic practices. *Annual review of sociology*, 24, 105–140.

Paris, R., 2002. International peacebuilding and the 'mission civilisatrice'. *Review of international studies*, 28, 637–656.

Pottier, J., 2002. *Re-imagining Rwanda, conflict, survival and disinformation in the late twentieth century.* Cambridge: Cambridge University Press.

Power, S., 2002. *'A problem from hell', America and the age of genocide.* New York: Harper Perennial.

Prunier, G., 1998. *The Rwanda crisis: history of a genocide.* 2nd revised ed. London: Hurst & Co.

Prunier, G., 2009. *Africa's world war, Congo, the Rwandan genocide, and the making of a continental catastrophe.* Oxford: Oxford University Press.

Scheper-Hughes, N., 2005. Between global bystander and global intervener. *Journal of human rights*, 4, 165–169.

Schwenkel, C., 2006. Recombinant history: transnational practices of memory and knowledge production in contemporary Vietnam. *Cultural anthropology*, 21 (1), 3–30.

Smith, J., 2006. Our memorial to 50,000 dead is no empty historic exercise. Debate around the Murambi genocide site in Rwanda is expected and necessary. *The Guardian*, 21 Nov. Available from: http://www.guardian.co.uk [Accessed 18 September 2009].

Steele, S.L., 2006. Memorialisation and the land of the eternal spring: performative practices of memory on the Rwandan genocide. Refereed paper delivered at PASSAGES: Law, Aesthetics, Politics, Melbourne, Australia, 13–14 Jul.

Storey, A., 2001. Structural adjustment, state power and genocide: the World Bank and Rwanda. Paper for presentation at the Conference on the Global Constitution of 'Failed States': Consequences for a New Imperialism?, Sussex, 18–20 Apr.

Straus, S., 2006. *The order of genocide, race, power and war in Rwanda*. Ithaca NY/London: Cornell University Press.

United Nations, 1999. Report of the independent inquiry into the actions of the United Nations during the 1994 genocide in Rwanda. 15 Dec. Available from: http://www.un.org/Docs/journal/asp/ws.asp?m=S/1999/1257 [Accessed 9 May 2011].

Uvin, P., 1998. *Aiding violence: the development enterprise in Rwanda*. West Hartford, Connecticut: Kumarian Press.

Uvin, P., 2001. Difficult choices in the new post-conflict agenda: the international community in Rwanda after the genocide. *Third world quarterly*, 22 (2), 177–189.

Verbeek, G., 2007. Structure of memory: Apartheid in the museum. *In*: H.E. Stolten, ed. *History making and present day politics: the meaning of collective memory in South Africa*. Uppsala: Nordiska Afrikainstitutet, 217–226.

Vidal, C., 2001. Les commemorations du génocide au Rwanda. *Les Temps Modernes*, 56 (613), 1–46.

Webley, R., 2004. *Report on Rwanda*. Berkeley, CA: War Crimes Study Center. Available from: http://socrates.berkeley.edu/~warcrime/Papers/webley-thesis.pdf [Accessed 4 February 2008].

Werbner, R., 1998. Smoke from the barrel of a gun: postwars of the dead, memory and reinscription in Zimbabwe. *In*: R. Werbner, ed. *Memory and the postcolony, African anthropology and the critique of power*. London: Zed Books, 71–102.

Williams, P., 2007. *Memorial museums: the global rush to commemorate atrocities*. Oxford/New York: Berg.

Young, J.E., 1993. *The texture of memory: holocaust memorials and meaning*. New Haven, CT/London: Yale University Press.

Zorbas, E., 2007. Keep out of our affairs: how the post-genocide government in Rwanda manages relations with donors. Paper presented at the 48th Annual International Studies Association Convention, Politics, Policy and Responsible Scholarship, Chicago, 28 Feb.–3 Mar.

Claims to the Past. A Critical View of the Arguments Driving Repatriation of Cultural Heritage and Their Role in Contemporary Identity Politics

Liv Nilsson Stutz

This article explores the role that the worldwide movement of repatriation of human remains and cultural heritage—from museums and other institutions to minorities and indigenous populations—plays in contemporary identity politics. Beyond the obvious positive outcomes of this process, including a significant democratization of the field of archaeology, the repatriation movement poses challenges, mainly because it relies on concepts such as past—present continuity that are sometimes subtly, sometimes not so subtly, problematic for legitimizing group identities and group claims to cultural heritage and human remains. It is argued that while archaeologists and anthropologists must continue to support the idea of increasing democratization of interpreting the past, they must also maintain the right to remain critical to all claims of the past by any particular group.

Introduction

Over the past three centuries, cultural collections in museums and universities worldwide have substantially grown, as ethnographic objects, 'curiosities', archaeological artefacts, biological specimens and human remains made their way into shelves, display cases and storage facilities. These collections were built up in large part through exchange, trade and scientific excavation, but also through raw theft (Fforde 2002, O'Neill 2006, Thomas 2000, Trigger 1989) and— reflecting a practice that continues illicitly today—buying of looted or stolen objects (e.g. Brodie and Walker Tubb 2002, Brodie *et al.* 2008, Renfrew 2000). Once established as museum collections, these ethnographic, archaeological and physical anthropological materials have provided a key set of material sources, which have inspired some and insulted and alienated others. Especially from the late nineteenth century onward, the disciplines of archaeology and anthropology, notably following the teachings of Franz Boas (1987), have widely seen their research as well as museum collections as serving the study of humanity in all its diversity (e.g. MacGregor 2009, de Montebello 2009, Appiah 2009). Yet, in the post-colonial and post-modern period, critical voices within these disciplines have argued that—especially when seen in retrospect—museum collections (and the academic discipline of archaeology) have facilitated a monopolization of discourse about the past and identity, by propagating a modernist and Western world view through its typologies and established orders; this monopoly over the past is widely seen as having been produced and reproduced as an ideology of domination (Bennett 1995, Cody Cooper 2008, Fforde 2004, McNiven and Russell 2005, but for a critique, see also Brown 2009, pp. 148–149). As Lynn Meskell puts it, 'The archaeology of power—to name, classify and domesticate—doubles as a means to obliterate, silence and negate other histories' (Meskell 1998, p. 5). The post-colonial and post-modern critique in archaeology has also emphasized that interpretations are always shaped, explicitly or implicitly, by contemporary political agendas, including nationalism and colonialism (Atkinson *et al.* 1996, Díaz-Anderu and Champion 1996, Fforde 2004, Fine-Dare 2002, Gathercole and Lowenthal 1990, Kohl and Fawcett 1995, Liebmann 2008, Meskell 1998, Thomas 2000, Trigger 1989). Clearly archaeology and anthropology, like all academic disciplines, provide a particular reflection of the values and ideologies of their times. It is therefore not surprising that in today's post-colonial, post-industrial, globalizing geopolitical climate, we see an intense questioning of the past and of museums and the collections they house. The most concrete political expression of this general questioning may be the rapid reverse movement of objects, which are leaving museum institutions—those historically fundamental symbols of modernizing colonial Western nations—as they are returned as *cultural heritage* to their communities of origin. The process is called *repatriation*, and it has become a global phenomenon.

The return of human remains and objects from museums and other collections to their communities of origin is typically viewed as a process of emancipation of previously oppressed groups. It is seen as a sign of democratization and as an important step on the path towards self-definition for groups that in the past were deprived from writing their own histories. These positive outcomes are undeniable, and yet the phenomenon is not unproblematic. The most often heard argument against repatriation concerns the loss of research material and the impact of imposing permanent interpretations of archaeological material. While this tension between 'saving data' and participating in a post-colonial archaeology or anthropology continues to receive a great deal of academic and media attention (Dalton 2008), the repatriation process brings to light some largely unexplored dimensions of identity construction in a post-colonial political setting (but see Bauer *et al.* 2007, Nilsson Stutz 2008, 2009). This article critically examines the theoretical foundations for the arguments that—sometimes implicitly, sometimes explicitly—are used to support repatriation of cultural heritage. These include the notions of past–present continuity, ownership of the past and of cultural heritage, right to culture and right to difference and essentialism—all concepts that have been deconstructed or critiqued in contemporary post-colonial anthropological and archaeological theory.

The purpose of this article is not to reject the process of repatriation, but to clarify the stakes involved. It is argued here that while repatriation may be the best possible negotiated outcome in many cases, it is nevertheless important to examine thoroughly the underlying arguments advanced by the stakeholders. In a contemporary moment when, in many contexts, the dividing lines are more blurred between West and Other, the Academy and Other, we see that social theory in anthropology and archaeology has come to emphasize the dynamic and hybrid nature of social identity—as an ever changing process of contestation, negotiation, domination and resistance. It is important to analyse and deconstruct political arguments that may simply seek to invert, rather than move beyond, the colonial order.

Repatriation, a Global Movement of Emancipation

Having taken off as part of the civil rights movement in the United States and Australia in the 1960s and 1970s (Bray 2001), repatriation as a process transcends the mere transfer of ownership of items and human remains from the museums back to their source communities. More than that, it constitutes a process of reconciliation and a strategy in which the communities of origin regain the right to define themselves, their history and identity (Fforde 2004, Hubert and Fforde 2002, Thornton 2002, Tsosie 1997). In the case of human remains, the process also allows for them to give their ancestors a lasting burial, which today is viewed by many as a case of right to religion (Hubert and Fforde 2002, Nagar 2002, Tsosie 1997, Riding In 2000, Riding In *et al.* 2004). The histories of museums and the disciplines of archaeology and anthropology are critically reviewed in this process, but, more importantly, their contemporary role is also renegotiated. From having held a position of authority, museums and science must now concede not only parts of their collections, but also their monopoly to interpret the past.

Repatriation has engaged numerous nation-states as well as indigenous peoples and minorities. It has rapidly become a global phenomenon. As such, it reflects a changed world order where formerly colonized and oppressed groups are gaining political influence in society, and where they can effectively exercise this influence by claiming control over their cultural heritage and the remains of their ancestors. A brief overview of the phenomenon points to its preponderance and diversity. A few countries, including the United States (Native American Graves Protection and Repatriation Act 1990) and Australia (the Aboriginal and Torres Strait Islander Heritage Protection Act 1984), have national legislation that regulates the process of repatriation to their indigenous populations. Israel has legislation that regulates the return for reburial of any human remains that are claimed as Jewish by the ultra-orthodox community (Nagar 2002). While most countries lack legislation to regulate reburial of human remains, claims are regularly negotiated on a case-by-case basis in order to accommodate public sensitivity defined in a majority cultural context. An example of this can be found in regulations developed in recent years in the United Kingdom.[1] Extra-legal repatriation agreements have also been reached between governments and minority groups such as indigenous Sami representatives in Finland, Norway and Sweden (Harlin 2008) or to Jewish congregations in Sweden (Orrenius 2005), the United Kingdom (Bergquist 2001, p. 187, Cox 1997, p. 9) and Spain (*New York Times* 2009). Recently, a claim from the Council of British Druids Order, a self-proclaimed ethnic religious group in the British Isles, seeking repatriation of the Neolithic remains (dated to have an age within the range of 4,000–5,700 years old) from the Alexander Keiller Museum at Avebury was denied (Thackray and Payne 2008, see also Sayer 2009). A special case may be seen with Greenland, where shortly after its partial independence in 1979, the semi-autonomous government initiated negotiations for the return of roughly 35,000 ethnographic and archaeological Inuit artefacts from the National Museum in Copenhagen (Grønnow and Lund Jensen 2008, but for a critique, see Lynge 2008). International repatriation is also increasing, and for the most part the process is not defined by legal treaties, such as the Convention on the Means of Prohibiting and Preventing the Illicit Import, Export and Transfer of Ownership of Cultural Property 1970,[2] but rather it is guided by policy statements, such as the ICOM (International Council of Museums) Code of Ethics for Museums (2004). In general terms the ICOM Code states that museums should be prepared to initiate dialogue for the return of cultural property to a country or people of origin (art. 6.2). The careful formulation states that the process should 'be undertaken in an impartial manner, based on scientific, professional and humanitarian principles as well as applicable local, national and international legislation, in preference to action at a governmental or political level (art. 6.2). Today it is not unusual for museums, often sanctioned by the nation-state of which they are part, to return cultural items after negotiations with indigenous communities and/or nation-states (for some diverse examples, please see Abungu 2008, Curtis 2008, Guerrero 2009, Herewini 2008, Munjeri 2009, O'Neill 2006, Wilson 2009). But, international repatriation requests are not always accommodated, and in the example of the Parthenon Friezes (the Elgin Marbles), the British Museum's refusal to return the world-famous antiquities to Athens is an enduring source of friction between the UK and Greece (Divari-Valakou 2008, Greenfield 1995, Merryman 1985, Webb 2002).

The purpose of repatriation varies greatly depending on the context. While repatriated cultural objects may be included in local or regional museum collections—as in the case of the Greenland Inuit (Grønnow and Lund Jensen 2008)—they are perhaps more often used in ceremonies and rituals as part of living cultural traditions. The human remains that are repatriated are often reburied, as the group requesting repatriation would seek to give their ancestors a lasting and proper burial. In the United States and Australia it is notable that repatriation legislation is far reaching, in the sense that the law allows for a complete transfer of ownership of the items. With the growth of national and international repatriation agreements being negotiated outside of formal legal frameworks, we see almost all conceivable variation in how the museum and the requesting party reach agreement. Some agreements have been highly restrictive over access to any further scientific study, but other agreements have favoured accommodation for the researchers to conduct last minute analyses and sample collection prior to final repatriation. Despite the contextual variability within the repatriation movement, there is a striking similarity in which the claims are made and in the ways in which the stakeholders define themselves. For example, the British Druids see themselves as an oppressed minority and an indigenous population to the British Isles and thus borrow their discourse from the indigenous debate regarding Native Americans. Similarly, the ultra-orthodox Jewish communities in Israel see the traditional right to rebury what they define as their ancestors in prehistory as an undisputed traditional and indigenous right on a par with that of aboriginal Australians.

Viewed in the light of how repatriation as a process redefines the authority of the scientific interpretation of the past and of past–present continuity, these arguments create a significant dilemma for archaeologists and biological anthropologists around the world, as they generate a field for potential abuse of the past to gain political advantage in the present. The situation begs the question of what the proper role and responsibility of the archaeologist and anthropologist should be in this situation. On the one hand, the repatriation process has positively democratized the production, management and representation of the material 'documents' of human diversity and the 'unwritten' human past, in the sense that it has given the opportunity for more people and groups to participate in knowledge production (see for example contributions in Swidler *et al.* 1997, Killion 2008). From this perspective, repatriation has levelled the playing field and benefitted all stakeholders, including the archaeologists and museum curators (Lippert 2008, Watkins 2003, p. 135). On the other hand, this inclusion of new voices in the process has also affected research and exhibitions in a restrictive way. Certain topics perceived as controversial (slavery, violence, cannibalism, mortuary rituals, etc.) or deemed uninteresting by the indigenous or minority communities involved may become less researched, either because the material remains can no longer be accessed, or because it would affect the relationships between researcher and those communities negatively (Brown 2009, p. 150).

It may not be surprising, then, that archaeologists and biological anthropologists have responded to the success of repatriation movements in diverse ways. In a wider political field, academics no longer have a monopoly over the authority of knowledge about a given society or particular region's prehistory. Given that historically this politically embedded monopoly of knowledge production emerged with the wholesale colonial plundering of archaeological and ethnographic treasures—ranging from monuments to textiles to human remains— the repatriation process is providing an opportunity for reconciliation between the different stakeholders. Here, many archaeologists and anthropologists are actively supporting repatriation policies, joining national governments and the representatives of minority groups (Watkins 2003, 2008a, 2008b, Ferguson 1996, Ferguson *et al.* 2000, Fine-Dare 2002, Dongoske 2000, Zimmerman 1989, McGuire 1989). Still, a large number of archaeologists and biological anthropologists have worriedly cautioned against the dangers of giving up access, usually permanently, to those rare sources of the unwritten histories of the past (Baker *et al.* 2001, Owsley and Jantz 2002, Swain 2007). These researchers argue that because science is constantly changing, current interpretations of these materials are likely to be revisited in the future, as new methods and new information become available. To return museum collections, they argue, makes re-study of the material practically impossible. This has consequences beyond the individual interests of the researcher. As one scientific interpretation is attached to a material in the process of facilitating repatriation, it tends to impose permanence on that particular interpretation. Future questioning and testing becomes impossible. We will see later how in the long term this can have political consequences.

The Powerful Past: Archaeology, the Past and Identity Politics

The past plays a central part in identity processes. A symbolic or material connection to the past situates and anchors the wider cultural context in which social identities are shaped; the past links one's identity to 'a world already defined' (Friedman 1994, pp. 117–118). The process of situating oneself in the world can be seen as the outcome of an engaged social agency of, often unconscious, selections from the past (Anico and Peralta 2009, p. 1). We select from our myths and histories the aspects which we, as a collective, feel comfortable with and to which we are able to connect. From this constructed social memory we anchor our sense of place in the world. Identity construction is, in other words, an ongoing collective dynamic social process, which relies on concepts of past–present continuity in a shared identity that today may be discussed in both cultural (symbolic) and biological (scientifically verifiable genealogical) terms. A much publicized example of the latter is the establishment of ancestry based on DNA analysis conducted on a group of African American celebrities in the *African American Lives* project (Gates Jr. 2009, for a critique, see Duster 2008). An uninterrupted cultural and biological link, imagined or 'real', between the people of the past and the contemporary community establishes a sense of kinship and provides an important place in the world. Ties to the past are symbolically represented. They are also significant for how individuals act to maintain their own social ties to the wider community. Repatriation as a process builds on a similar social production of symbolic and genealogical kinship. At the same time it also reproduces the notion that the social relationships have a tangible source and reason for being. As such, repatriation can become a very effective and desired tool for identity production for the group that is involved in it.

Indeed, to become effective, identities must have some kind of materiality (Anico and Peralta 2009, p. 1). Re-use and appropriation of material culture—including monuments and artefacts—can support a political strategy for creating legitimacy and continuity through time. Such practices of re-use and appropriation of the material past may be traced archaeologically to prehistory (Bradley 2002, Artelius 2004). Following an ethno-symbolic view of human communities, concrete material remains assure a durability and 'common consciousness' for ethnic groups that can last through periods of rapid change and endow each community with 'a distinctive symbolic repertoire' (Smith 2009, p. 25). The shared, 'real' and mythological past, and the material remains that provide a concrete connection to that past play a central role in this production of shared identity and community. As the provider of tangible but often ambiguous material remains of that past, archaeology has historically been an attractive partner in this process. A brief overview of the past two centuries of archaeology clearly shows that interpretations of material remains often are highly ideological, and that archaeology has been skilfully used in various political discourses (Trigger 1984). Archaeology played a central role in the statebuilding processes of many European countries during the nineteenth and early twentieth centuries. The most notorious example of the excesses of nationalist archaeology is that of Germany in the 1930s. Archaeology—both the act of excavation and the uncovered prehistoric objects and monuments themselves—provided a source of inspiration for the growing fascist movement of the Third Reich (Arnold and Hassmann 1995, Eickhoff 2005, Halle 2005). Archaeology offered material symbols—experienced as earthly, real and convincing by German citizens—of the deep and pure historical roots of the united and superior German people. In a less dramatic way perhaps, but still following nationalist agendas, the prehistoric or early historical material remains of nations ranging from Great Britain (Fowler 1987), Greece (Hamilakis 2003) and Sweden (Hagerman 2006), to Israel (Silberman 1995, Abu El-Haj 2001), Guatemala (Joyce 2003) and Japan (Fawcett 1995) have been used to project publicly ideas of a deep, united past for the nation's people. More recently, archaeology and archaeological artefacts have been used ostensibly politically to reinforce transnational identities, such as a common identity for the European Union (see contributions in Graves *et al.* 1996, Gröhn 2004, pp. 144–180, Kristiansen 2008, Pluciennik 1996). In many cases, archaeology was exploited to legitimize claims to political, military or artistic achievement, superior character, or innate ability. Beyond these more intangible values, claims to a material past can also have corresponding, larger material consequences. By appropriating the past, a group of people can redefine not only the right to history, but also to material resources such as territory. Recent examples of this can be seen in the events leading up to the civil war in the former Yugoslavia (Verdery 1999, p. 18); the role of archaeology in determining the presence of Israelite and Jewish remains in prehistory and history that provide a link to the contemporary state (Abu El-Haj 2001, Finkelstein and Silberman 2001, Silberman 1993, 1995, Greenberg 2009); and for that matter, the ways in which recent occupation by indigenous groups in

South Africa was denied by the state during apartheid in order to evict them from what was constructed as 'pristine nature' in national parks (Meskell and Masuku Van Damme 2008). While clearly diverse, these cases are all examples of contexts where history, prehistory and material remains have been heavily utilized to make claims to territory and other resources.

It may be especially relevant to reinforce a sense of community when significant change takes place. The archaeologist Bjørnar Olsen has discussed how archaeology and anthropology and their pivotal roles in both nationalism and colonialism during the nineteenth and early twentieth centuries may be understood by their links to modernity (Olsen 2001, p. 43). Modernity, he argues, came to entail 'two seemingly conflicting philosophical positions', by combining a stress on rationality and progress with a romantic nostalgia for the past. Archaeology as *a science of the past* embodied both. The changes brought about by modernity in many European states during the nineteenth century—including the erosion of traditional peasant folk culture and the extensive social uncertainty generated by agricultural land reform, industrialization, urbanization and Transatlantic migration—created a widely expressed and deeply felt sense of loss in Europe, a sense that something important was slipping away and had to be preserved and rescued. 'To preserve the past became part of preserving the present, of preserving our own identity' (Olsen 2001, p. 43). This eagerness to preserve something that was slipping away motivated the collection of the cultural heritage of rural communities as modern society expanded. Here, we can start to understand the role of archaeology in the national states in Europe during the nineteenth and early twentieth century.

At the same time, archaeology and anthropology also became employed in colonialist projects. Through the study of the material culture of the colonized, along with anthropological studies of their bodies (dead and alive), archaeology and anthropology provided the colonial project with its scientific legitimacy. The colonized peoples were defined as 'primitive'. They were either in need of the 'help to evolve' that contact with the colonizers graciously afforded them, or they were seen as incapable of change and doomed to extinction (Trigger 1989, pp. 110–147, Thomas 2000, pp. 44–51, 64–70, Scheper-Hughes 2001). When archaeologists came across what seemed to be evidence of a more sophisticated past culture, such as the ruins in Great Zimbabwe (Trigger 1989, pp. 130–135, Vale 1999) or the mounds of the Southeast and Midwest of the United States (Thomas 2000, pp. 124–129, Trigger 1989, pp. 105–109, 119–129), the archaeological monuments were attributed to people other than the current indigenous populations. These 'more sophisticated people', according to the interpretations of colonial and racist archaeology, were thought necessarily to have been replaced by the current occupants at some point in history or prehistory (a common understanding of the mound-builders of North America). Alternatively, their superiority had vanished as they degenerated through interracial mixing with what was seen as the biologically and culturally inferior ancestors of the current indigenous population. This was a particularly popular idea in the nineteenth century European interpretation of Great Zimbabwe. Cultural heritage was, in other words, put in the service of the colonial political agenda. The pattern described by Olsen above was also exported within the colonial framework, where archaeologists, ethnographers, anatomists and others who employed themselves in 'salvage ethnography' collected items from what they perceived as cultures destined to disappear. While some today emphasize the close entanglement of this practice with colonial politics and even genocide (Phillips and Johnson 2003, Thomas 2000, Fine-Dare 2002), others take a more forgiving stand and propose to view it in its context as a form of ineffective act of resistance, or a 'weak response to genocide' (Scheper-Hughes 2001, p. 14).

Although nationalist and colonial archaeologies of the nineteenth and early twentieth centuries were products of the same process of modernity, one great difference existed between the nationalist and colonial contexts. While the political and cultural establishments in various European nations celebrated (although sometimes in a patronizing way) their own cultural histories—proudly presenting the material remains of their ancestors in national museums across the continent—the cultural heritage (and sometimes even the people themselves) of the colonized was shipped off to foreign cities, often included in ethnographic collections or even museums of natural history, the latter being an act denying them even their humanity (e.g. Blanchard *et al.* 2008). The result of these practices can be seen with stark clarity in the fact that today the most prestigious collections of material culture of African history and prehistory can only be viewed in European and North American museums (Abungu 2008, pp. 36–37).

Here, we find a key to one of the central problems within the repatriation debate today. Based on the different experiences in the nationalist and colonial context, the idea of appropriation of cultural heritage by a particular group has different implications. While nationalism and colonialism inextricably shaped a process in which the dominating political power achieved hegemony over interpreting the material remains of the past, there were also significant differences in the exploitation of cultural heritage within the colonialist and nationalist projects (especially in interpretation and positioning of indigenous-ness), and these different experiences still influence the repatriation debate today. In the nationalist context, the European majority population defined itself as indigenous and heirs of the land. 'The Other' was historically identified as an intruder and included minorities such as Jews, Roma and Sami, who were seen as impure elements that threatened or disturbed the continuous histories and genealogies of the nation (see e.g. Catomeris 2004, Hagerman 2006, Ljungström 2004, Olsen 2001, Schanche 2002, Sellevold 2002). In this political, academic and historical context, the appropriation of cultural heritage by a particular group was associated with reactionary movements such as ethno-nationalism and nationalism. In the colonial context, on the other hand, 'the Other' was identified with the indigenous, which was simultaneously exoticized, naturalized and defined as inferior, in order to legitimize the political project of colonialism (Trigger 1989, pp. 110–147, Thomas 2000). From this perspective, the recent indigenous claims to cultural heritage have become inscribed into a progressive history of emancipation. Today, the debate on repatriation is clearly dominated by these voices from a post-colonial context. However, it may be important to consider the nationalist experience and learn from the abuses committed in its name. The full complexity of the history of archaeology and of the phenomenon of repatriation may best be understood if we make the effort to integrate all of these different and sometimes conflicting narratives, as we address claims to culture in the future.

Fresh Shoots and Deep Roots—Archaeology and Contemporary Identity Processes

Today, archaeologists would be the first to acknowledge that their interpretations are subjective and that the discipline is bound to be highly political. If nothing else, history has taught us how effectively the discipline can be manipulated by various wider political interests. The overwhelming majority of archaeologists today would also distance themselves from the way in which archaeology was abused by nationalist and colonialist interests in the nineteenth and early twentieth centuries. Outside of the discipline, however, archaeology is still perceived as telling 'true' stories about the past, and, because of this, it still maintains a much wider authority, but it also becomes vulnerable to abuse. Today's world is different from that of the nineteenth century, when archaeology was shaped into an academic discipline. As the colonial and nationalist systems have been replaced by a post-colonial world, identity politics have changed and with them so has the use of the past (Anico and Peralta 2009). Today we live in a world that is simultaneously characterized by trends towards both homogenization—with more extensively globally shared, resonant cultural references—and fragmentation, seen through the increasing impact of multi-cultural societies, hybrid cultures and diaspora cultures (Eriksen 1997, 2002, Eriksson *et al.* 2005, p. 40). Migration and globalization have led to a redefinition of cultural identity. This is especially clear in the old nation-states in Europe, which no longer can rely on a perceived sense of homogeneity. While migration always has contributed to constant change in population dynamics and cultural processes in European nation-states, we now have a public debate about these processes and about how to redefine our identities to conform to this notion of dynamic multiculturalism. Today, transnational migration and diaspora culture are visible social phenomena inextricably linked to post-colonial identity politics and the ongoing tangled dynamic of tensions between post-colonial nation-states, former colonial powers, Cold War powers and, more recently, post-9-11 powers. In this contentious, often violent, and highly interconnected global political context, the past is always present, acting as a node of gravitation. The material past—shaped by archaeological and anthropological collections, sites and studies—still defines a place where these new or rediscovered identities can be situated and legitimized. People still rely on past–present continuity to situate themselves in the world. Here, the

POLITICAL CULTURE, SOFT INTERVENTIONS AND NATION BUILDING

political relevance of repatriation may be brought more clearly into focus, as we compare how politicized claims to the past have been used in building post-colonial national identities with how the global repatriation movement has been—and remains—largely driven by indigenous communities (Eriksen 2002). Repatriation claims have become a symbol of post-colonial emancipation. They are, by definition, a 'good thing', and are rarely deconstructed and questioned from a political position. But anybody who has seen the negative consequences of exclusive appropriation of culture must immediately ask themselves if this blanket approach is entirely responsible. In this section I will outline some of the ideological underpinnings of the repatriation discourse and through concrete examples illustrate the potential range of their consequences.

Who Owns the Past?

In our contemporary contentious political climate the material past has become a contested commodity. As more and more people are engaging in cultural heritage politics, the past and its material culture have become something that can be claimed by particular stakeholders as a form of property (Brown 2003, 2009). While the flaws of the old system of Western hegemony and an academic monopoly on the 'truth' may be widely acknowledged, the current response is not unproblematic. The repatriation movement relies on the idea that cultural heritage belongs to the descendants of the people that once produced it. Only they, it is argued, can decide the fate of these remains. This challenges the idea of cultural heritage belonging to all of humanity and limits access to the objects—for research, consultation, inspiration and so on. At a more funda-mental level it is also often argued that because of the past–present continuity that provides a crucial link between a contemporary group and a historical past in which an object was created, a particular contemporary group has a better understanding and insight into the object and its history. This idea is fundamental for the ideologies that state that, for example, an indigenous group has better understanding of their past than an outside academic. This may be true in many cases. However, it becomes problematic to endorse this view as a fundamental principle. How does this affect, for example, the opportunities for immigrants to relate to the history of their new homeland (Holtorf 2010), for minorities to engage in majority histories, or for men to become engaged with women's studies? How does this view of exclusive ownership of the local and historic past by indigenous groups (minorities *and* majorities) affect their place in the world? For archaeology to reproduce this idea may actually alienate us from the contemporary world characterized by a mix of identities including migrants, hybrid cultures and diaspora cultures.

Even if we would embrace this problematic principle, we would still have to face the challenges of establishing the past–present continuity. What may immediately appear as a technicality begins—upon closer inspection—to reveal a series of contested ideological underpinnings. The Native American Graves

Protection and Repatriation Act (NAGPRA), which since 1990 has regulated repatriation to Native Americans from museums and other institutions in the United States, is a case in point. In order to make a legally proper claim it must be established that there is an 'affiliation' between the claimant and the historic or prehistoric group from which the item originated (for more details, see Ousley *et al.* 2005). In other words, past–present continuity must be shown empirically. In some cases this is relatively easy—for example, when direct descendants claim the remains of a deceased relative for reburial, or when items from well-documented historic periods are claimed. But affiliation as a concept goes beyond immediate kinship and ownership. It can be projected far back in time and is decided on the principle of preponderance of evidence from a range of different sources—including geographical, kinship, biological, archaeological, anthropological, linguistic, folkloric, oral traditional, historical or other relevant information or expert opinion. From an archaeological point of view, these connections can become difficult to establish beyond a reasonable doubt. This is particularly the case when the remains are prehistoric, and where the archaeological understanding of the past does not correspond to a Native American claimant group's traditional knowledge. The conflict that ensued between different stakeholders after the remains of a 9,200-year-old skeleton washed out of a river bank in Kennewick in Washington State in 1996 illustrates this dilemma and the political consequences (Burke *et al.* 2008, Gardell 2003, pp. 149–151, 281–283, Gerstenblith 2002, Owsley and Jantz 2002, Watkins 2008b). In cases like these the scientific understanding of the world is challenged by a traditional understanding, and it is often difficult to find a satisfactory compromise. The solution in museums, as Michael Brown has pointed out, 'is to present their views side by side without attempting to reconcile them' (Brown 2009, p. 150). We can compare this extremely careful response from the scientific community to the debate on creationism and intelligent design vs evolution, where no museum of natural science would be equally generous in supporting the alternative voices on the subject. Yet, in the NAGPRA repatriation process, the stakes are higher for museums. Educational exhibits are no longer seen as requiring authentic ancient objects to convey a legitimate message (whether it is one of compromise and multivocality or not). Yet, according to NAGPRA, the establishment of affiliation means that the ownership of ethnographic collections or human bones is permanently transferred from the museum to the Native American claimant group. For archaeology the stakes may be especially high. While the discipline today is based on the understanding that our interpretations change over time, as new theories, perspectives, methods and knowledge are added to our engagement with the past, it is still perceived by others as simply providing hard, immutable facts about the past. Any decision that is made about cultural affiliation in a repatriation case today, and that is sanctioned by an archaeologist or archaeological institution, may be viewed by Native American groups, or a wider public as objective truth. Moreover, after the items are repatriated this affiliation can no longer be questioned, often for both practical and ideological reasons. By imposing an effective permanence on our interpretations, we limit the possibilities for future questioning of these items and their history. While this general awareness of the impermanence of our understanding of the world probably should not be the argument that calls into question all cases of repatriation, it should nevertheless inspire us to remain vigilant and critical to claims to cultural heritage. As we will see next, these claims can be used for very different purposes.

Repatriation, Recognition and Post-Colonial Nation-Building

Repatriation of cultural items constitutes one of the most powerful and most far reaching efforts acknowledging and articulating diverse indigenous identities within a common movement. The act of removing items from storage facilities and display cases and returning them to their original group is a manifestation of a changed power relationship, and it constitutes an act of recognition and respect for the culture from which these items were once taken. Beyond the expression of respect and potential reconciliation, repatriation offers the tools for self-determination to people who have experienced that this right was taken from them in the colonial past. From this perspective, repatriation can be seen as integral to what Charles Taylor has termed the 'politics of recognition' (Taylor 1992, see also Jenkins 2008). Taylor argues that since identity is shaped by other people's recognition or absence of recognition, the right to self-determination is the foundation of liberation and must be seen as a human right (Taylor 1992; for more details, see also Eriksson *et al.* 2005, p. 41, see also Barkan 2002, pp. 16–17). When applied to archaeology and anthropology, this means that repatriation of cultural heritage and human remains becomes a necessary step towards post-colonial liberation, since it is only through the revision of the histories written by past archaeologists and anthropologists, and through a release of control over the cultural heritage and the human remains, that such freedom and liberation from the colonial past can be achieved. This view is of fundamental importance for repatriation proponents, for whom this right to self-definition carries much deeper significance than the scientific value of the items that are being returned. By regaining control over the physical remains of the past, these peoples now control not only their place in the material world, but also—through the recognition of their claim to these items—the right to truly define their identity and control their history. It is not a coincidence that repatriation claims are becoming more successful at a moment when colonial history is being re-written and the rights of indigenous peoples are gaining recognition, both nationally and internationally. States that recognize the rights of their indigenous communities tend to take on an intermediary but active role in supporting claims by indigenous minority groups within their borders. This involvement by the state on behalf of recognized minorities is often essential for the indigenous groups' successful repatriation claims (please see the ICOM Code of Ethics discussed above). International repatriations that involve the support of the state tend to create a sense of common cause for the indigenous people and the nation that acts in collaboration with them. One example of this is the return of *toi moko* (preserved tattooed heads of Māori people)—from various museums across the world—to the Te Papa Tongarewa Museum of New Zealand (Curtis 2008, Herewini 2008). This museum is one of the most striking post-colonial national museums today, exhibiting both historical and contemporary Māori culture and the culture of later arrived New Zealanders. It is explicitly profiled as 'representative of New Zealand's culturally diverse society' and pronounces on it homepage that it 'makes a significant contribution toward the key government goal *"To Strengthen National Identity and Uphold the Principles of the Treaty of Waitangi"'* (http://www.tepapa.govt.nz). The museum becomes a statement for how indigenous New Zealand and colonial history are both woven into the imagery of the contemporary national state. Beyond the sense of shared destiny, it is also clear that the Māori have achieved a position of power and respect that has allowed them to further their agenda, something which is an overarching goal for the outcome of repatriation claims made by minorities and/or indigenous peoples (Hole 2007). The goodwill negotiations between indigenous groups such as the Greenland Inuit and the National Museum of Denmark and the Te Papa Tongarewa Museum and diverse museums around the world appear to have led to a striking, inclusive democratization of the past, and as such they constitute examples of what most parties agree to be successful repatriations. It should also be clear that these repatriations are part of ongoing political and ideological processes. It is still often overlooked that the right to culture can be put to different uses. Anthropologist Thomas Hylland Eriksen has pointed out that 'cultural pleas' can serve very different political ideologies and agendas, employed by both 'political leaders of hegemonic majorities as well as by spokesmen of weak minorities' (Eriksen 1997, p. 54). In the post-colonial setting, we tend to associate invocations of culture with resistance. Yet, 'the political implications of such claims cannot be generalised because culture may be called upon to legitimise reactionary projects as easily as progressive ones' (Cowan *et al.* 2001, p. 10). Repatriation to indigenous minorities who assert the right to culture can result from and contribute to a discourse about native identity that is grounded in essentialism, ethno-nationalism and exclusive claims to the past (Nilsson Stutz 2008, 2009).

Examples of this can be seen in the use of the past in some of the states that emerged with the mid-twentieth-century retreat of colonial powers. Here, the formerly colonized people began to take back the same key right: that of defining their culture and history. Exercising this right is not only a strategy for indigenous minorities to assert themselves in today's world, but has also become an important component of post-colonial nation-building, where identity has depended 'not only on international recognition but on sub-national self-promotion' (Vale 1999, p. 405). Post-independence politicians and leaders often found that they needed to 'counter the false impressions disseminated by a century of colonialist media' (Vale 1999, p. 405). 'Sub-national self-promotion' has been achieved through exploitation of archaeology and the material remains of the past, helping to build a convincing connection between the power and

POLITICAL CULTURE, SOFT INTERVENTIONS AND NATION BUILDING

authority of the new state and the nation's legitimate cultural link to the past. There is nothing that automatically shields these new uses of the past from familiar forms of abuse.

For example, Bruce Trigger has pointed out that, as many former African colonies gained independence, the colonial archaeology was replaced by a nationalist archaeology (Trigger 1984), with post-colonial leaders exploiting more the materiality, ancientness or permanence of monuments and artefacts, and relying less on well-documented archaeological facts, in utilizing cultural heritage to cement and wield power. In the case of Great Zimbabwe, the understanding and representation of the site took a dramatic turn with independence, as the site's history was re-written in nationalist language. Great Zimbabwe is presented as anchoring the deep historical roots of the modern state of Zimbabwe, defining a depth of cultural continuity that is singled out as unique in Africa. To drive home the point, President Robert Mugabe's government supported reconstructing a nineteenth-century village of the local tribe, the Shona, as a living museum adjacent to the ruins. This arrangement reinforced the material representation of past–present continuity. The underlying political agenda became obvious when Mugabe claimed a family lineage to a namesake who allegedly once ruled in the area; Mugabe did not mention that his claimed ancestors came to the region more than two centuries after the collapse of the city (Vale 1999, p. 404).

Of course, African post-colonial states are not alone in creating nationalist archaeologies to replace colonialist projects. Under President Saddam Hussein, Iraq engaged in a dramatic post-colonial re-reading of Mesopotamian cultural heritage (Vale 1999). Through ambitious recreations of Ancient Babylonian monuments, Saddam Hussein sought to boost national Iraqi pride by celebrating a golden age of the past, while at the same time creating a place that could attract tourists. Saddam Hussein more directly embellished his own legitimacy, claiming political affiliation to Nebuchadnezzar, 'the powerful king who conquered Jerusalem, destroyed the Second Temple, and carried thousands of Jews into captivity' (Vale 1999, p. 400). He thus sought to present himself as the rightful descendant and heir of the political power in the Middle East. Such symbols of past–present continuity also constituted a popular appeal to pan-Arab aspirations, thus giving Saddam Hussein substantial political capital within a regional geopolitical context. When considering the exploitation of cultural heritage in authoritarian post-colonial nations, the prospects of repatriation may be considered more critically. Saddam Hussein could have plausibly claimed the famous Ishtar Gate to be returned from the Pergamon Museum in Berlin, but it is very unlikely that such a request would have been granted. Robert Mugabe could, according to the same logic, use the repatriation movement to strengthen his claim to personal affiliation with Great Zimbabwe and the political legacies such a connection could provide. I emphasize that this is a hypothetical suggestion, made for the purposes of critically examining the general notion of repatriation. Here, such negotiations for repatriation were never initiated. But the central point that I am making is that the lack of critical inquiry of the political dimension of repatriation as a cultural intervention linked to identity politics lays the field open to this kind of abuse should the occasion arise. In this light, it is also interesting to consider the myriad ways that repatriation could influence national and ethnic identity politics in post-9/11 and post-Saddam Iraq. More broadly, the role of archaeology in post-colonial statebuilding can be seen in a wide range of geographic and political contexts as different as Zimbabwe, Iraq (Vale 1999), Honduras (Joyce 2003), and Israel (Abu El-Haj 2001, Greenberg 2009). In all of these examples, cultural heritage yields particularly effective symbols, where the nation, or strong interest groups within the nation (Greenberg 2009), seeks to assert ancient, valid, tangible roots, as they seek dominance in political discourse among disparate interest groups. As described above, repatriation and reburial legislation in Israel—passed in 1994 (Nagar 2002, Watzman 1996)—has the effect of asserting, within a traditional religious framework, the pre-eminence of Jewish history in a modern, diverse post-colonial nation that is defined as a Jewish homeland in the dominant discourse. If we are critical of the use of archaeology in nationalist discourses during the nineteenth and early twentieth centuries in Europe, and we are aware of the abuses that may be committed in its name—as a tangible and deceptively 'objective' proof of historical narratives, then we must remain critical as we see similar nationalist discourses emerge in post-colonial contexts as well. This move towards nationalism and ethno-nationalism within the repatriation movement has up to today received strikingly little attention in the debate, and the critique is often simply rejected as irrelevant.

Repatriation and Indigenous Peoples and Minorities: The Right to Difference

The most painful struggles for repatriation are probably those concerning minorities and/or indigenous peoples who direct claims to the state within whose borders they reside. Not all indigenous groups have achieved legal or practical recognition of the role of repatriation, as Native American, Australian Aborigine, Māori and Greenland Inuit groups have obtained. In many other cases minority claims are not necessarily supported by the state. Instead, these claims become part of a struggle for civil and human rights for a particular minority within their own country. Critics have said that these claims to culture have tended to replace the struggle for other rights, such as healthcare and education, which have simply been abandoned due to lack of political progress (Fraser 1997, p. 2). However, it is also crucial not to underestimate the importance that this right to the past and self-definition has for many communities (Forsman 1997). Because these groups do not have complete sovereignty within their states, and their state is the party with whom they enter into negotiations, their arguments of the right to culture are complemented with arguments of the right to difference, i.e. the right to have different values, sensitivities and needs than the majority population. Seen in this perspective, the practice of repatriation becomes a strategy through which groups can extricate themselves from the dominating culture and establish a self-centred autonomy (Friedman 1994, p. 132). Within the right to difference discourse it is not unusual to see elements of essentialism, and the repatriation debate is no exception. It is common to see arguments for a difference in the way indigenous peoples or minorities as a group relate to their ancestors, a different view on burial and a different view of the value of science. The arguments are often expressed in sweeping statements about indigenous people that position them as *essentially* different from Westerners in general and archaeologists in particular (Deloria 1999a, 1999b, Shown Harjo in Riding In *et al.* 2004, Riding In 2000, White Deer 1997). These discourses that are founded on dichotomization create an artificial boundary between the West and indigenous societies, which in turn may be reduced to stereotypes. It is difficult to disentangle whether the claims are examples of what Cowan and colleagues have called 'strategic essentialism' (Cowan *et al.* 2001, p. 10, see also Eriksson *et al.* 2005, p. 43), or if they reflect an ontic essentialism that truly embraces the concept. No matter the intent, the discourse contributes to reproducing the idea of essential differences between different 'types' of people or cultures (see also Nilsson Stutz 2009). While these ideas may be seen as strengthening the sense of identity within a group, they may also be viewed as counterproductive for the relationships between groups. Basically, the reproduction of these ideas makes understanding and connection across the dividing line more difficult to achieve. For the indigenous groups themselves the use of essentialist arguments is not without risk. Olsen has pointed out that the use of strategic essentialism can be to the detriment also for the indigenous group since it tends to 'reinforce a reactionary museum image so long forced upon them by outside scholars and politicians (...). It attributes to them an unchanging essence, freezing them forever as always-the-same "traditional societies"' (Olsen 2001, p. 50). For archaeology and anthropology the essentialist component of this discourse constitutes an ethical dilemma. The deconstruction of the concept of essentialism constituted a significant move away from the darkest aspects of the histories of the disciplines, including their contributions to scientific racism and legitimization of colonialism. Does an engagement with these discourses today constitute a legitimization and reproduction of similar ideas?

Conclusion: The Stakes ... Beyond the Loss of Data

Repatriation is situated at the nexus of contemporary identity processes, including the debates about right to culture and right to difference. It resonates with debates about post-colonial identity politics, but it transcends the theoretical discussions as it also constitutes a practical transaction with concrete consequences, as permanence is imposed on the scientific interpretations regarding affiliation and cultural significance of the items that are returned. We have seen that cultural heritage is used in identity processes, and we have also seen how it has been abused in the past as part of nationalist and colonialist discourses. Today we emphasize an inclusive dialogue in cultural heritage politics, but as we do so we still cling to the concept of past–present continuity as the foundation of right to culture. While colonial and nationalist archaeologies were produced historically by the same European cultures, today the post-colonial situation in which repatriation is taking place tends to divorce the national from the former colonial. This makes sense in terms of aspirations for independence, but, with repatriation in particular, requiring a negotiated agreement between museums (legacy colonial institutions) and former colonized groups or nations, where they agree over past–present continuity and the scientific and cultural legitimacy of the repatriation claim, this attempt at reconciliation by cultural descendants of colonizers may encourage recapitula-tion of the cultural and biological essentialism that underlies nationalist and colonialist archaeologies. As a principle this excludes other groups than the descendants of that culture. In a world that is increasingly dominated by hybrid cultures, diaspora cultures and transnational migration, the past–present paradigm for culture heritage politics may come to constitute a real problem. How, for example, do we include recently arrived groups in a local cultural heritage? The dominating model within the repatriation debate today, which builds largely on the colonial experience, assumes that the indigenous is always the weaker party. This model is not transferrable to contexts where immigrants are marginalized, such as in many of the European nation-states, where growing groups of immigrants experience discrimination and exclusion, and where right-extremist political elements appropriate the local or 'national' prehistory to claim continuity to the past. It may also not always be the most responsible approach in contexts where new post-colonial nation-states are formed, and where one ethnic group may appropriate the cultural heritage and use it to legitimize a dominant position over other ethnic groups. We need to ask ourselves what consequences a nationalist discourse that builds on past–present continuity has for statebuilding efforts today, and especially what implications they may have for the future of those states.

It has sometimes been pointed out that struggles for the right to culture have replaced the struggle for social rights (Fraser 1997). While the symbolic gain in the repatriation of thousands of human remains and cultural items from museums in the United States may have had a considerable healing effect on the communities to which they were returned, it was probably also overall less costly for the United States government than to live up to its responsibilities for providing quality healthcare and education to Native Americans. We should be especially critical when repatriation becomes effectively divorced from other political processes of development and seems to replace other rights struggles.

Ultimately, the discussion about repatriation also touches upon very difficult issues of identities, how we view ourselves and, to an equal extent, how we view others. Most academics would probably agree that to capitulate to overt essentialism brings us to a path of divergence and separation. By enforcing the idea of cultural difference we may inadvertently enforce essentialism as a model for how we view human diversity. It is my firm belief that we instead must strive towards a sense of shared humanity that transcends cultural difference and that is built on mutual respect and identification. Repatriation has greatly improved the relationships between archaeologists and anthropologists and indigenous people and minorities. It remains an important tool for reconciliation, emancipation and democratization. It is now time to move this relationship forward. Archaeologists and anthropologists must find a way to handle repatriation while simultaneously avoiding a recapitulation or simple inversion of power relationships between colonizer and colonized, central state and local community, ethnic majority and ethnic minority. The main question becomes how to encourage dialogue, education and tolerance, and clarify the difference between nationalist/colonialist projects and right to culture aspirations, while still maintaining the ability to speak up about the potential dangers of essentialism.

Acknowledgements

I want to thank the Swedish Research Council for funding my research on repatriation discourses.

Notes

1   In 2005, English Heritage and the Church of England collaborated to establish a document entitled: *Guidance for best practice for treatment of human remains excavated from Christian burial grounds in England,* which now constitutes a reference for archaeological practice with regards to excavation and reburial.
2   The UNESCO Convention on the Means of Prohibiting and Preventing the Illicit Import, Export and Transfer of Ownership of Cultural Property 1970, binds states who have ratified it to return cultural property that was illegally obtained from another state. As an agreement between states, it gives no specific rights to minorities and indigenous groups per se. Moreover, it can only be applied to acts committed after the document was ratified, which means that older collections (i.e. the great majority of museum collections) are not concerned by the agreement.

References

Abu El-Haj, N., 2001. *Facts on the ground. Archaeological practice and territorial self-fashioning in Israeli society.* Chicago, IL: University of Chicago Press.

Abungu, G.O., 2008. 'Universal museums': new contestations, new controversies. *In*: M. Gabirel and J. Dahl, eds. *UTIMUT. Past heritage—future partnership. Discussions on repatriation in the 21st century.* Copenhagen: IWGIA, Document No. 122, 32–42.

Anico, M. and Peralta, E., eds, 2009. *Heritage and identity. Engagement and demission in the contemporary world.* Museum Meanings. London: Routledge.

Appiah, K.A., 2009. Whose culture is it? *In*: J. Cuno, ed. *Whose culture? The promise of museums and the debate over antiquities.* Princeton, NJ: Princeton University Press, 71–88.

Arnold, B. and Hassmann, H., 1995. Archaeology in Nazi Germany: the legacy of the Faustian bargain. *In*: P. Kohl and C. Fawcett, eds. *Nationalism, politics and the practice of archaeology.* Cambridge: Cambridge University Press, 70–81.

Artelius, T., 2004. Minnesmakarnas verkstad. Vikingatida bruk av äldre gravar och begravningsplatser. *In*: Å. Berggren, S. Arvidsson and A.-M. Hållands, eds. *Minne och Myt—konsten att skapa det förflutna.* Lund: Nordic Academic Press, 99–120.

Atkinson, J.A., Banks, I. and O'Sullivan, J., eds, 1996. *Nationalism and archaeology.* Glasgow: Cruithne Press.

Baker, B., Varney, T., Wilkinson, R., Anderson, L. and Liston, M., 2001. Repatriation and the study of human remains. *In*: T. Bray, ed. *The future of the past: archaeologists, Native Americans, and repatriation.* New York: Taylor and Francis, 69–90.

Barkan, E., 2002. Amending historical injustices. The restitution of cultural property—an overview. *In*: E. Barkan and R. Busch, eds. *Claiming the stones. Naming the bones. Cultural property and the negotiation of national and ethnic identity.* Los Angeles: The Getty Research Institute, 16–46.

Bauer, A., Lindsay, S. and Urice, S., 2007. When theory, practice and policy collide, or why do archaeologists support cultural property claims? *In*: Y. Hamilakis and P. Duke, eds. *Archaeology and capitalism. From ethics to politics.* Walnut Creek, CA: Left Coast Press, 45–58.

Bennett, T., 2005. *The birth of the museum. History, theory and politics.* London: Routledge.

Bergquist, A., 2001. Ethics and the archaeology of world religions. *In*: T. Insoll, ed. *Archaeology and world religion.* London: Routledge, 182–192.

Blanchard, P., Bancel, N., Boëtsch, G., Deroo, E., Lemaire, S. and Forsdick, C., eds, 2008. *Human zoos. Science and spectacle in the age of the colonial empires.* Liverpool: Liverpool University Press.

Boas, F., 1987. *Anthropology and modern life.* Mineola, NY: Dover Publications.

Bradley, R., 2002. *The past in prehistoric societies.* London: Routledge.

Bray, T., 2001. American archaeologists and Native Americans. A relationship under construction. *In*: T. Bray, ed. *The future of the past. Archaeologists, Native Americans and repatriation.* London: Garland Publishing, 1–5.

Brodie, N. and Walker Tubb, K., eds, 2002. *Illicit antiquities: the theft of culture and the extinction of archaeology.* London: Routledge.

Brodie, N., Kersel, M.M., Luke, C. and Walker Tubb, K., 2008. *Archaeology, cultural heritage, and the antiquities trade.* Gainesville, FL: University Press of Florida.

Brown, M.F., 2003. *Who owns native culture?* Cambridge, MA: Harvard University Press.

Brown, M.F., 2009. Exhibiting indigenous heritage in the age of cultural property. *In*: J. Cuno, ed. *Whose culture? The promise of museums and the debate over antiquities.* Princeton, NJ: Princeton University Press, 145–164.

Burke, H., Smith, C., Lippert, D., Watkins, J. and Zimmerman, L., eds, 2008. *Kennewick Man. Perspectives on the ancient one.* Walnut Creek, CA: Left Coast Press.

POLITICAL CULTURE, SOFT INTERVENTIONS AND NATION BUILDING

Catomeris, C., 2004. *Det ohyggliga arvet. Sverige och främlingen genom tiderna.* Stockholm: Ordfront.

Cody Cooper, K., 2008. *American Indians protest museum policies and practices.* Lanham, MD: AltaMira Press.

Cowan, J.K., Dembour, M.-B. and Wilson, R., 2001. *Culture and rights. Anthropological perspectives.* Cambridge: Cambridge University Press.

Cox, M., 1997. Crypt archaeology after Spitalfields: dealing with our recent dead. *Antiquity,* 70, 8–10.

Curtis, N., 2008. Thinking about the right home—repatriation and the University of Aberdeen. *In*: M. Gabirel and J. Dahl, eds. *UTIMUT. Past heritage–future partnership. Discussions on repatriation in the 21st century.* Copenhagen: IWGIA, Document No. 122, 44–54.

Dalton, R., 2008. No burial for 10,000-year-old bones. University of California denies request for repatriation of remains. *Nature,* 455, 1156–1157.

Deloria, V. Jr., 1999a. Ethnoscience and Indian realities. *In*: B. Deloria, K. Foehner and S. Scinta, eds. *Spirit and reason. The Vine Deloria Jr reader.* Golden, CO: Fulcrum Publishing, 63–71.

Deloria, V. Jr., 1999b. Indians, archaeologists and the future. *In*: B. Deloria, K. Foehner and S. Scinta, eds. *Spirit and reason. The Vine Deloria Jr reader.* Golden, CO: Fulcrum Publishing, 72–77.

De Montebello, P., 2009. And what do you propose should be done with those objects? *In*: J. Cuno, eds. *Whose culture? The promise of museums and the debate over antiquities.* Princeton, NJ: Princeton University Press, 55–70.

Díaz-Anderu, M. and Champion, T., eds, 1996. *Nationalism and archaeology in Europe.* Boulder, CO: Westview Press.

Divari-Valakou, N., 2008. Revisiting the Parthenon—national heritage in a global age. *In*: M. Gabirel and J. Dahl, eds. *UTIMUT. Past heritage—future partnership. Discussions on repatriation in the 21st century.* Copenhagen: IWGIA, Document No. 122, 116–121.

Dongoske, K., 2000. NAGPRA a new beginning, not the end, for osteological analysis—a Hopi perspective. *In*: D. Mihesuah, eds. *Repatriation reader. Who owns American Indian remains?* Lincoln: University of Nebraska Press, 282–293.

Duster, T., 2008. Deep roots and tangled branches. *Chronicle of higher education.* Available from: http://www.geneticsandsociety.org/article.php?id=3908 [Accessed 24 July 2009].

Eickhoff, M., 2005. German archaeology and National Socialism. Some historiographical remarks. *Archaeological dialogues,* 12 (1), 73–90.

English Heritage and the Church of England, 2005. *Guidance for best practice for treatment of human remains excavated from Christian burial grounds in England.*

Eriksen, T.H., 1997. Multiculturalism, individualism and human rights: romanticism, the enlightenment and lessons from Mauritius. *In*: R. Wilson, ed. *Human rights, culture and context. Anthropological perspectives.* London: Pluto Press, 49–69.

Eriksen, T.H., 2002. *Ethnicity and nationalism. Anthropological perspectives.* 2nd ed. London: Pluto Press.

Eriksson, C., Eriksson Baaz, M. and Thörn, H., 2005. *Globaliseringens kulturer. Den postkoloniala paradoxen, rasismen och det mångkulturella samhället.* Nora: Nya Doxa.

Fawcett, C., 1995. Nationalism and postwar Japanese archaeology. *In*: P. Kohl and C. Fawcett, eds. *Nationalism, politics and the practice of archaeology.* Cambridge: Cambridge University Press, 232–246.

Ferguson, T.J., 1996. Native Americans and the practice of archaeology. *Annual review of anthropology,* 25, 63–79.

Ferguson, T.J., Anyon, R. and Ladd, E.J., 2000. Repatriation at the Pueblo of Zuni: diverse solutions to complex problems. *In*: D. Mihesuah, ed. *Repatriation reader. Who owns American Indian remains?* Lincoln: University of Nebraska Press, 239–265.

Fforde, C., 2002. Collection, repatriation and identity. *In*: C. Fforde, J. Hubert and P. Turnbull, eds. *The dead and their possessions. Repatriation in principle, policy and practice*. One World Archaeology. London: Routledge, 25–46.

Fforde, C., 2004. *Collecting the dead. Archaeology and the reburial issue*. London: Duckworth.

Fine-Dare, K.S., 2002. *Grave injustice. The American Indian repatriation movement and NAGPRA*. Lincoln: University of Nebraska Press.

Finkelstein, I. and Silberman, N.A., 2001. *The Bible unearthed: archaeology's new vision of ancient Israel and the origin of its sacred texts*. New York: Free Press.

Forsman, L., 1997. Straddling the current: a view from the bridge over clear salt water. *In*: N. Swidler, K.E. Dongoske, R. Anyon and A.S. Downer, eds. *Native Americans and archaeologists. Stepping stones to common ground*. Walnut Creek, CA: AltaMira Press, 105–111.

Fowler, D., 1987. Uses of the past: archaeology in the service of the state. *American antiquity*, 52 (2), 229–248.

Fraser, N., 1997. *Justice interruptus: critical reflections on the 'postsocialist' condition*. London: Routledge.

Friedman, J., 1994. *Cultural identity and global processes*. London: Sage Publications.

Gardell, M., 2003. *Gods of the blood. The pagan revival and white separatism*. Durham, NC: Duke University Press.

Gates Jr, H.L., 2009. *In search of our roots: how 19 extraordinary African Americans reclaimed their past*, New York: Crown Publishing.

Gathercole, P. and Lowenthal. D., eds, 1990. *The politics of the past*. One World Archaeology. London: Unwin Hyman.

Gerstenblith, P., 2002. Cultural significance and the Kennewick skeleton: some thoughts on the resolution of cultural heritage disputes. *In*: E. Barkan and R. Bush, eds. *Claiming the stones. Naming the bones. Cultural property and the negotiation of national and ethnic identity*. Los Angeles: Getty Publications, 162–197.

Graves, P., Jones, S. and Gamble, C., 1996. *Cultural identity and archaeology. The construction of European communities*. London: Routledge.

Greenberg, R., 2009. Towards an inclusive archaeology in Jerusalem: the case of Silwan/the City of David. *Public archaeology*, 8 (1), 35–50.

Greenfield, J., 1995. *The return of cultural treasures*. 2nd ed. Cambridge: Cambridge University Press.

Gröhn, A., 2004. *Positioning the Bronze Age in social theory and research contexts*. Acta archaeologica Lundensia. Series in 8°, 47. Stockholm: Almqvist & Wiksell International.

Grønnow, B. and Lund Jensen, E., 2008. Utimut: repatriation and collaboration between Denmark and Greenland. *In*: M. Gabirel and J. Dahl, eds. *UTIMUT. Past heritage—future partnership. Discussions on repatriation in the 21st century*. Copenhagen: IWGIA, document No. 122, 180–191.

Guerrero, B.A., 2009. Repatriation of cultural properties: the Peruvian experience. *Museum international*, 61 (1–2), 241–242.

Hagerman, M., 2006. *Det rena landet. Om konsten att uppfinna sina förfäder*. Stockholm: Prisma.

Halle, U., 2005. Archaeology in the Third Reich. Academic scholarship and the rise of the 'lunatic fringe'. *Archaeological dialogues*, 12 (1), 91–102.

Hamilakis, Y., 2003. Lives in ruins: antiquities and national imagination in modern Greece. *In*: S. Kane, ed. *The politics of archaeology and identity in a global context*. Boston, MA: Archaeological Institute of America, 51–78.

Harlin, E.-K., 2008. Repatriation as knowledge sharing—returning the Sámi cultural heritage. *In*: M. Gabirel and J. Dahl, eds. *UTIMUT. Past heritage—future partnership. Discussions on repatriation in the 21st century*. Copenhagen: IWGIA, Document No. 122, 192–200.

Herewini, T.H., 2008. The Museum of New Zealand Te Papa Tongarewa (Te Papa) and the repatriation of Kōiwi Tangata (Mäori and Moriori skeletal remains) and Toi Moko (mummified Maori tattooed heads). *International journal of cultural property*, 15, 405–406.

Hole, B., 2007. Playthings for the foe: the repatriation of human remains in New Zealand. *Public archaeology*, 6 (1), 5–27.

Holtorf, C., 2010. A European perspective on indigenous and immigrant archaeologies. *World archaeology*, 41 (4), 672–681.

Hubert, J. and Fforde, C., 2002. Introduction: the reburial issue in the twenty-first century. *In*: C. Fforde, J. Hubert and P. Turnbull, eds. *The dead and their possessions. Repatriation in principle, policy and practice*. One World Archaeology. London: Routledge, 1–16.

Jenkins, T., 2008. Dead bodies: the changing treatment of human remains in British museum collections and the challenge to the traditional model of the museum. *Mortality*, 13 (2), 105–118.

Joyce, R., 2003. Archaeology and nation building: a view from Central America. *In*: S. Kane, ed. *The politics of archaeology and identity in a global context*. Boston, MA: Archaeological Institute of America, 79–100.

Killion, T.W., ed., 2008. *Opening archaeology. Repatriation's impact on contemporary research and practice*. Santa Fe, NM: School for Advanced Research Press.

Kohl, P. and Fawcett, C., eds, 1995. *Nationalism, politics and the practice of archaeology*. Cambridge: Cambridge University Press.

Kristiansen, K., 2008. Do we need the 'archaeology of Europe'? *Archaeological dialogues*, 15 (1), 5–25.

Liebmann, M., 2008. Introduction: the intersections of archaeology and postcolonial studies. *In*: M. Liebmann and U.Z. Rizvi, eds. *Archaeology and the postcolonial critique*. Lanham, MD: AltaMira Press, 1–20.

Lippert, D., 2008. Not the end, not the middle, but the beginning. Repatriation as a transformative mechanism for archaeologists and indigenous peoples. *In*: C. Colwell-Chanthaphonh and T.J. Ferguson, eds. *Collaboration in archaeological practice. Engaging descendant communities*. Lanham, MD: AltaMira Press, 119–130.

Ljungström, O., 2004. *Oscariansk antropologi. Etnografi, förhistoria och rasforskning under sent 1800-tal*. Uppsala: Gidlunds förlag.

Lynge, A., 2008. Sharing the hunt. Repatriation as a human right. *In*: M. Gabirel and J. Dahl, eds. *UTIMUT. Past heritage—future partnership. Discussions on repatriation in the 21st century*. Copenhagen: IWGIA, Document No. 122, 78–82.

MacGregor, N., 2009. To shape the citizens of 'that great city, the world'. *In*: J. Cuno, ed. *Whose culture? The promise of museums and the debate over antiquities*. Princeton, NJ: Princeton University Press, 39–54.

McGuire, R., 1989. The sanctity of the grave: white concepts and American Indian burials. *In*: R. Layton, ed. *Conflict in the archaeology of living traditions*. London: Unwin & Hyman, 167–184.

McNiven, I. and Russell, L., 2005. *Appropriated pasts. Indigenous peoples and the colonial culture of archaeology*. Lanham, MD: AltaMira Press.

Merryman, J.H., 1985. Thinking about the Elgin Marbles. *Michigan law review*, 83 (8), 1880–1923.

Meskell, L., 1998. *Archaeology under fire. Nationalism, politics and heritage in the eastern Mediterranean and Middle East*. London: Routledge.

Meskell, L. and Masuku Van Damme, L.S., 2008. heritage ethics and descendant communities. *In*: C. Colwell-Chanthaphonh and T.J. Ferguson, eds. *Collaboration in archaeological practice. Engaging descendant communities*. Lanham, MD: AltaMira Press, 131–150.

Munjeri, D., 2009. The reunification of a national symbol. *Museum international*, 61 (1–2), 241–242.

Nagar, Y., 2002. Bone reburial in Israel: legal restrictions and methodological implications. *In*: C. Fforde, J. Hubert and P. Turnbull, eds. *The dead and their possessions. Repatriation in principle. Policy and practice*. London: Routledge, 87–90.

New York Times, 2009. Graves disturbed, Jewish group says. *New York Times*, 29 May.

Nilsson Stutz, L., 2008. Caught in the middle—an archaeological perspective on repatriation and reburial. *In*: M. Gabirel and J. Dahl, eds. *UTIMUT. Past heritage—future partnership. Discussions on repatriation in the 21st century*. Copenhagen: IWGIA, Document No. 122, 84–98.

Nilsson Stutz, L., 2009. Archaeology, identity, and the right to culture. Anthropological perspectives on repatriation. *Current Swedish archaeology*, 15–16, 157–172.

Olsen, B., 2001. The end of history? Archaeology and the politics of identity in a globalized world. *In*: R. Layton, P.G. Stone and J. Thomas, eds. *Destruction and conservation of cultural property*. London: Routledge, 42–54.

O'Neill, M., 2006. Repatriation and its discontents: the Glasgow experience. *In*: E. Robson, L. Treadwell and C. Gosden, eds. *Who owns objects? The ethics and politics of collecting cultural artefacts*. Oxford: Oxbow Books, 105–128.

Orrenius, N., 2005. Här kan Dombrowsky få vila i frid. *Sydsvenska Dagbladet*, 10 Feb.

Ousley, S.D., Billeck, W.T. and Hollinger, R.E., 2005. Federal repatriation legislation and the role of physical anthropology in repatriation. *Yearbook of physical anthropology*, 48, 2–32.

Owsley, D.W. and Jantz, R.L., 2002. Kennewick Man—a kin? Too distant. *In*: E. Barkan and R. Bush, eds. *Claiming the stones. Naming the bones. Cultural property and the negotiation of national and ethnic identity*. Los Angeles, CA: Getty Publications, 141–161.

Phillips, R.B. and Johnson, E., 2003. Negotiating new relationships. Canadian museums, First Nations and cultural property. *In*: J. Torpey, ed. *Politics and the past. On repairing historical injustices (world social change)*. Lanham, MD: Rowman and Littlefield, 149–167.

Pluciennik, M., 1996. A perilous but necessary search: archaeology and European identities. *In*: J.A. Atkinson, I. Banks and J. O'Sullivan, eds. *Nationalism and archaeology*. Cruithne Press: Glasgow, 35–58.

Renfrew, C., 2000. *Loot, legitimacy and ownership: the ethical crisis in archaeology*. London: Duckworth.

Riding In, J., 2000. Repatriation. A Pawnee's perspective. *In*: D.A. Mihesuah, ed. *Repatriation reader. Who owns Native American Indian remains?* Lincoln: University of Nebraska Press, 106–120.

Riding In, J., Seciwa, C., Harjo, S.S., Echo-Hawk, W.R. and Tsosie, R., 2004. Protecting Native American human remains, burial grounds, and sacred places: panel discussion. *Wicazo Sa review: a journal of Native American studies*, 19 (2), 169–183.

Sayer, D., 2009. Is there a crisis facing British burial archaeology? *Antiquity*, 83, 199–205.

Schanche, A., 2002. Sami skulls, anthropological race research and the repatriation question in Norway. *In*: C. Fforde, J. Hubert and P. Turnbull, eds. *The dead and their possessions. Repatriation in principle, policy and practice*. London: Routledge, 47–58.

Scheper-Hughes, N., 2001. Ishi's ashes Ishi's brain. Anthropology and genocide. *Anthropology today*, 17 (1), 12–18.

Sellevold, B.J., 2002. Skeletal remains of the Norwegian Saami. *In*: C. Fforde, J. Hubert and P. Turnbull, eds. *The dead and their possessions. Repatriation in principle, policy and practice*. London: Routledge, 59–62.

Shown Harjo, S., 2004. Contribution in J. Riding In, C. Seciwa, S. Shown Harjo W. Echo-Hawk, Protecting Native American human remains, burial grounds, and sacred places panel discussion. *Wiazo Sa review*, 19 (2), 169–183.

Silberman, N.A., 1993. *A prophet from amongst you. The life of Yigael Yadin: soldier, scholar, and mythmaker of modern Israel*. Reading, MA: Addison-Wessley Publishing Company.

Silberman, N.A., 1995. Promised lands and chosen peoples: the politics and poetics of archaeological narrative. *In*: P. Kohl and C. Fawcett, ed. *Nationalism, politics and the practice of archaeology*. Cambridge: Cambridge University Press, 249–262.

Smith, A.D., 2009. *Ethno-symbolism and nationalism. A cultural approach*. London: Routledge.

Swain, H., 2007. The value of human remains in museum collections. An international symposium held at the Museum in Docklands, London, March 2007. *Public archaeology*, 6 (3), 193–197.

Swidler, N., Dongoske, K.E., Anyon, R. and Downer, A.S., eds, 1997. *Native Americans and archaeologists. Stepping stones to common ground*. Walnut Creek, CA: AltaMira Press.

Taylor, C., 1992. *Multiculturalism and 'the politics of recognition'*. Princeton, NJ: Princeton University Press.

Thackray, D. and Payne, S., 2008. Draft report on the request for the reburial of human remains from the Alexander Keiller Museum at Avebury. English Heritage.

Thomas, D.H., 2000. *Skull wars. Kennewick Man, archaeology and the battle for Native American identity*. New York: Basic Books.

Thornton, R., 2002. Repatriation as healing the wounds of the trauma of history: cases of Native Americans in the United States. *In*: C. Fforde, J. Hubert and P. Turnbull, eds. *The dead and their possessions. Repatriation in principle, policy and practice*. London: Routledge, 17–24.

Trigger, B., 1984. Alternative archaeologies: nationalist, colonialist, imperialist. *Man*, New Series, 19 (3), 355–370.

Trigger, B., 1989. *A history of archaeological thought*. Cambridge: Cambridge University Press.

Tsosie, R., 1997. Indigenous rights and archaeology. *In*: N. Swidler, K.E. Dongoske, R. Anyon and A.S. Downer, eds. *Native Americans and archaeologists, stepping stones to common ground*. Walnut Creek, CA: AltaMira Press, 64–76.

Vale, L.J., 1999. Mediated monuments and national identity. *The journal of architecture*, 4, 391–408.

Verdery, K., 1999. *The political lives of dead bodies. Reburial and postsocialist change*. New York: Columbia University Press.

Watkins, J., 2003. Archaeological ethics and American Indians. *In*: L. Zimmerman, K.D. Vitelli and J. Hollowell-Zimmer, eds. *Ethical issues in archaeology*. Walnut Creek, CA: AltaMira Press, 129–141.

Watkins, J., 2008a. The repatriation arena: control, conflict and compromise. *In*: T.W. Killion, ed. *Opening archaeology. Repatriation's impact on contemporary research and practice*. Santa Fe, NM: School for Advanced Research Press, 161–177.

Watkins, J., 2008b. Who's right and what's left of the middle ground. *In*: M. Gabirel and J. Dahl, eds. *UTIMUT. Past heritage—future partnership. Discussions on repatriation in the 21st century*. Copenhagen: IWGIA, Document No. 122, 100–106.

Watzman, H., 1996. Threat of ban hangs over Israeli archaeology. *Nature*, 382, 659.

Webb, T., 2002. Appropriating the stones: the 'Elgin Marbles' and English national taste. *In*: E. Barkan and R. Busch, eds. *Claiming the stones. Naming the bones. cultural property and the negotiation of national and ethnic identity*. Los Angeles, CA: The Getty Research Institute, 51–96.

White Deer, G., 1997. Return to the sacred. Spirituality and the scientific imperative. *In*: N. Swidler, K.E. Dongoske, R. Anyon and A.S. Downer, eds. *Native Americans and archaeologists. Stepping stones to common ground*. Walnut Creek, CA: Altamira Press, 37–43.

Wilson, C., 2009. Implications and challenges of repatriating and reburying Ngarrindjeri Old People from the 'Edinburgh Collection'. *Museum international*, 61 (1–2), 241–242.

Zimmerman, L.J., 1989. Made radical by my own: an archaeologist learns to accept reburial. *In*: R. Layton, ed. *Conflict in the archaeology of living traditions*. London: Unwin & Hyman, 60–67.

Legal Documents and Policy Documents

Aboriginal and Torres Strait Islander Heritage Protection Act 1984, Act No. 79 of 1984 as amended.

English Heritage and the Church of England, *Guidance for best practice for treatment of human remains excavated from Christian burial grounds in England*, 24 January 2005.

ICOM Code of Ethics for Museums, re-titled and revised by the General Assembly of ICOM in Seoul, 8 October 2004.

Native American Graves Protection and Repatriation Act, 16 November 1990 (Public Law 101-601; 25 U.S.C. 3001 *et seq.*)

UNESCO Convention on the Means of Prohibiting and Preventing the Illicit Import, Export and Transfer of Ownership of Cultural Property, Paris, 14 November 1970.

A Many-Cornered Thing: The Role of Heritage in Indian Nation-Building

Brian Hole

India is a large and extremely diverse multination state that is constantly faced with the challenge of maintaining its unity. In the past two decades the Hindu nationalist movement has become a significant factor in Indian politics, and has systematically leveraged heritage to create communal tensions. This has resulted in short-term political gain, but is also tied to longer-term goals of establishing a homogenously Hindu state in South Asia. This article argues that instead of being in decline, this movement is actually progressively expanding, and that the case of Ayodhya is only one part of a much larger programme in which heritage academics play a significant role, and that their collective actions will be pivotal to the future stability of the country.

Introduction

There is an assumption behind most nationalist theories of India that as a concept it is indivisible, and that while highly diverse it is nonetheless comprised of sufficient unifying factors to naturally function as an autonomous whole (Prakash 1992, p. 360). This is also the view of Amartya Sen, who stresses a long history of tolerance of diversity, leading to a naturally secular state (Sen 2005, p. 17). Time and again throughout the world's history, however, the divergent will of various ethnic groups has proved unstoppable. This was recognized by Rabindranath Tagore, who in 1917 described the greatest challenge for India as being:

> ...the problem of the world in miniature. India is too vast in its area and too diverse in its races. It is many countries packed in one geographical recepta-cle...India...being naturally many, yet adventitiously one, has all along suffered from the looseness of its diversity and the feebleness of its unity. A true unity is like a round globe; it rolls on, carrying its burden easily. But diversity is a many-cornered thing which has to be dragged and pushed with full force. (Tagore 1917, p. 124)

It is too narrow a view to say that the Indian state is able to achieve stability principally through a secular approach, with which it is able to define and maintain the idea of a single nation and from which it then derives its legitimacy. In reality, as noted by Tagore, much 'dragging and pushing' of various elements of the population is required in order to achieve this. While stemming mainly from Europe in the early twentieth century, the ideas of Hannah Arendt provide a useful lens with which to view and interpret the mechanism of nation-building in India.

According to Arendt in *The Origins of Totalitarianism*, mechanisms inherent to the nation-state ensure that national minorities not fitting its strict and coherent vision of 'the nation' are effectively relegated to a 'stateless' condition (Arendt 1951, p. 290, Butler and Spivak 2007, p. 31). Such minorities enter what Arendt, in *The Human Condition*, terms the private as opposed to the public world; they are effectively neither able to participate in the politics of the state, nor to fully receive protection from it (Arendt 1958, p. 221). This is essentially an alternative strategy to pure secularism, which enables the state to manage a very diverse population by making it politically less so. I contend that in the case of India, while a serious attempt at a secular state has been made on the surface, Arendt's ideas more closely describe the actual mechanisms that the state has effectively deployed to this end since independence. This is, however, a delicate situation, as Arendt recognized in *The Origins of Totalitarianism*:

> The great danger arising from the existence of people forced to live outside the common world is that they are thrown back, in the midst of civilisation, on their natural givenness, on their mere differentiation. (Arendt 1951, p. 302)

In cases where a majority religious identity comes to dominate government and the pretence of secularism is dropped (as is progressively happening), this could mean that stateless communities would come to view themselves as separate nations along ethnoreligious lines. None of the possible outcomes of such situations, for example repression, expulsion or secession, are likely to occur non-violently, or without affecting the stability of both the state and those neighbouring it. Over time, any change to the approach that India and groups within it take to secular governance and nation-building may well have an impact upon its ability to maintain order among its national minority groups, and ultimately upon its very integrity.

I would like to advance the argument that the use and interpretation of heritage plays a highly significant role in this process, and will thus directly help to determine the future form of the Indian nation-state. To do this, this article looks at how concepts of an Indian nation have arisen, and at the state of Indian nationalism today. This is followed by a review of how heritage academics (archaeologists and historians) have been involved with nationalist theories and movements and what their impact has been. Importantly, this review draws together a range of recent events that have not been clearly linked in other studies. Looking then to the future, the potential for Indian archaeology to counter right-wing nationalism is assessed, along with the potential internal and international consequences if it does not choose this path.

Nationalism and Heritage

The concept of India as a single territory goes back possibly as far as the third century BC, with the Maurya Empire (Kulke and Rothermund 2004, p. 61). Since then, many other kingdoms and empires have occupied a large part of the same area, including the Chalukyas, the Vijayanagara Empire, the Delhi Sultanate and the Mughal Empire. Despite being territorially unified under the British, the Government of India Act 1935 created separate electorates based on religion, creating the conditions for the rise of sectarian nationalism and eventually leading to partition in 1947, a policy aptly described as 'divide and leave' (Thakur 1993, p. 647).

The India that emerged from partition fits Kymlicka's terminology of a 'multination state' made up of 'national minorities', which he defines as '...the coexistence within a given state of more than one nation, where "nation" means a historical community, more or less institutionally complete, occupying a given territory or homeland, sharing a distinct language and culture' (Kymlicka 1995, p. 11). As Kymlicka points out, such states can only survive if each national minority both has an allegiance to the greater political community of the multination state, and, at the very least, they '...view themselves for some purposes as a single people' (Kymlicka 1995, p. 13). These were the questions being asked of the new citizens of India in 1947.

As when Massimo D'Azeglio in 1861 had said that 'We have made Italy. Now we must make the Italians' (Beales and Biagni 1971, p. 3), so the new generation of Indian leaders were now faced with the same challenge. Writing of his youth in 1946, Jawaharal Nehru explained that the middle class he belonged to were very much the product of the British system and its views, which they now sought to challenge:

> New forces arose that drove us to the masses in the villages, and for the first time, a new and different India rose up before the young intellectuals who had almost forgotten its existence, or attached little importance to it. It was a disturbing site, not only because of its stark misery and the magnitude of its problems, but because it began to upset some of our values and conclusions. So began for us the discovery of India as it was...(Nehru 1946, p. 50)

Describing the conclusions he came to about Indian identity, he wrote that:

> I was also fully aware of the diversities and diversions of Indian life, of classes, castes, religions, races, different degrees of cultural development. Yet I think that a country with a long cultural background and a common outlook on life develops a spirit that is peculiar to it and that is impressed upon all its children, however much they may differ among themselves. (Nehru 1946, p. 52)

Serving as India's first prime minister from 1947–64, Nehru pursued a vision of a secular Indian state that would not be bound by class stratification (Sen 2005, p. 204). In order to achieve this, religion was explicitly excluded as an organizational factor, and there was to be no one official national language, despite the dominance of Hindi. The Indian states were reorganized according to language in 1963, which Brass has described as the 'most successful and balanced nationality policy which has been pursued in either India or the Soviet Union' (Brass 1991, p. 314).

Following Nehru's death, it was during the three terms that Indira Gandhi served as prime minister between 1966 and 1984 that sectarian nationalism once more began to take hold in India. Indira Gandhi pursued interventionist policies designed to eliminate state governments run by rival parties, often appealing to voters on the basis of religious issues. This was one of the causes of an increase in sectarian violence and the rise of secessionist movements in Assam, Kashmir, Mizoram, Nagaland and the Punjab (Brass 1991, p. 318). Eventually this became her downfall, and she was assassinated in retaliation for putting down a Sikh separatist movement in the Punjab that she had helped to create.

In particular, her concessions to conservative Muslim demands had the effect of strengthening right-wing Hindu claims that despite government pretences of secularism, Muslims were receiving preferential treatment. The main party to benefit from this was the Bharatiya Janata Party (BJP), which went from only two seats in the Lok Sabha (lower house of the parliament) in 1984 to 85 seats in 1989. The BHP is the political party of the Hindu nationalist movement, also referred to as Hindutva or the Sangh Parivar. Other organizations that fit under this umbrella are the Vishwa Hindu Parishad (World Council of Hindus, VHP) and the Rashtriya Swayamsevak Sangh (National Self-Help Association, RSS).

These policies were largely continued by Rajiv Gandhi, culminating in the Shao Bano case in 1987, in which the government amended the constitution to specifically deny Muslim women rights to maintenance support following divorce, which until then had been granted to all other Indian women. This was seen as 'a watershed event' by the BJP, which galvanized popular Hindu sentiment against what was perceived as Muslim fanaticism (Ludden 2005, p. 225).

Thus, by the start of the 1990s the policies of India's government had drifted some way from those of secularism and equality under Nehru. With the VHP and BHP on the rise, a coordinated programme of right-wing Hindu policies and propaganda was ready to be deployed, in which nationalist claims to heritage have played a significant role.

India has been known for its archaeological heritage since the earliest days of the discipline, with Palaeolithic artefacts having been discovered as early as 1863 in Chennai (Chakrabarti 2006, p. 1). Numerous travellers and British officials had reported on the archaeological richness of India, but it was however the discovery of the Indus civilization by Pandit Daya Ram Sanhi in 1920 that first made a major difference to Indian perceptions of their own past in national terms:

> ... the discovery of the Indus civilization made India a respected member of the small number of lands that gave birth to true civilized life. In India, at least, the discipline of archaeology has served the country well, allowing it to take its rightful place as one of the oldest and most interesting regions of human endeavour. (Paddayya 1995, p. 143)

POLITICAL CULTURE, SOFT INTERVENTIONS AND NATION BUILDING

With partition in 1947 the main Indus sites of Harappa and Mohenjo-Daro became part of Pakistan, so Indian archaeologists' attention was quickly focussed on finding further examples of the civilization within their new borders in order not to lose this distinction. At the same time, Indian historians began to write their own works, which naturally tended to be anti-colonial in nature, with the aim of refuting British claims that India had always been a diverse collection of ethnic groups that could only be governed as a whole by outsiders, and that any evidence of a highly developed civilization was the result of external influences. In order to portray the past as more indigenous, homogenous and independent, the new historians sought to show that it originated with an essentially Hindu culture. They continued to work with the periods defined by the British, emphasizing that the Indian nation had begun with a golden age of Hinduism, and then later been oppressed and exploited by the Muslims and the British. While this began as an anti-colonial stance, it was also to become a great support for Hindu nationalists, and as Prakash (1992, p. 360) points out, this perspective '...had and continues to have deadly implications for a multiethnic country such as India'.

From independence onwards the Archaeological Survey of India (ASI) and a growing number of Indian university archaeology departments have produced a large body of excellent, scientifically balanced work that has greatly enriched our knowledge of the highly diverse, common history and prehistory of South Asia, a point that will be taken up again later in this article. At the same time however, various actors with more narrow nationalist aims have taken a much more selective and exclusive approach. While they are a minority, their voices are often heard the loudest because their well-publicized claims are aimed to coincide with major political or communal issues of the day, and being highly emotive, they often create 'facts' that go unscrutinized by the wider public, what Prakash has termed 'worlding the Third World' (1992, p. 382).

As often follows the gaining of independence, the first targets were the immediately departed British, with many prominent colonial monuments being demolished (Rao 1994, p. 154). Another symbol of an earlier colonial period, the Somanatha temple in Gujarat had been destroyed in the eleventh century in a raid by the Muslim Mahmud of Ghazni. In 1951 its ruins were cleared despite the protests of historians and archaeologists, and a new temple was built as a statement of freedom from foreign rule. This was a nationalist project, undertaken in order to celebrate the founding of a new and predominantly Hindu state, and for this reason it was strongly opposed by Nehru:

> While it is easy to understand a certain measure of public support in this venture, we have to remember that we must not do anything that comes in the way of our State being secular...There, are, unfortunately, many communal tendencies at work in India today and we have to be on our guard against them. It is important that Governments should keep the secular and non-communal ideal always before them. (quoted in Thapar 2004, pp. 189–190)

Despite Nehru's opposition, the communal focus on the past began to grow, with the main antagonist being the Hindutva movement. A central facet of Hindu

POLITICAL CULTURE, SOFT INTERVENTIONS AND NATION BUILDING

nationalism is to portray India as culturally homogenous (i.e. Hindu), whereby anyone or anything that does not fit this definition is cast as illegitimate and inferior. Many strategies involving heritage have been employed to achieve this, including attempting to claim the earliest occupation of the sub-continent, attacking 'illegitimate' heritage sites and defending Hindu ones, misrepresenting the history of cultural interaction, and attempting to misinform the public through the media and school textbooks. We will look at each of these approaches in turn, both in terms of how they have been achieved, and what impact they have had on the stability of the Indian nation-state.

The most well known example of nationalist heritage destruction in India is that of Ayodhya in Uttar Pradesh, but this has been a major catalyst for similar events in other parts of India as well, and examples will be given from Gujarat, Maharashtra and Karnataka.

Ayodhya is a town in the Faizabad district of Uttar Pradesh, with a population of around 75,000. Although identified today with the mythical city of the same name in the great epic poem the Ramayana, research has shown that the modern Ayodhya was given its name in the fifth century by the Gupta king Skanda Gupta, in order to gain political prestige (Gopal *et al.* 1990, p. 77). Since around the middle of the nineteenth century, a belief had begun to spread among some Hindus that the Babri Masjid (mosque) in Ayodhya had been built on top of a temple to the god Rama, on the very spot of his birth. In 1949 a group of local Hindus broke into the mosque and deposited Hindu idols, at which point the local magistrate had the mosque locked and made unavailable for worship. The situation remained tense but mostly uneventful for the next 30 years.

During this time, several archaeological investigations of Ayodhya and the surrounding area were made, including one in the 1970s by the eminent archaeologist B.B. Lal very near to the Babri Masjid, which uncovered little more than what appeared to be a section of a fortification (Lal 1976–77, p. 52), rousing little interest. This is significant, as Lal was dedicated to searching for evidence of the Ramayana epic, and as such would not simply ignore the potential discovery of one of its major locations.

By the 1980s the uneasy tension that had prevailed at the site was finally ignited by the communal tensions being stirred up by Indira Gandhi's adminis-tration, and in 1984 a movement known as the Ram Janmabhumi (Birthplace of Rama) campaign was started, with the aim of claiming the site for Hindus. This was supported by the VHP and the RSS, and received a major boost when the BJP decided to actively support it in order to broaden their popularity. The decision to politicize the association of the mosque with Rama is not a random one. As Pollock (1993, p. 282) has noted, the Ramayana is a text that involves significant 'demonization of the other', and is therefore very suitable for stirring up communal tensions. This is something that the BJP has actively played upon, even producing travelling theatrical productions in which the BJP as Rama fights against rival parties in the form of the menacing and immoral Ravanna (Gillan 2003, p. 385). In 1985 the campaign began to demand that the mosque be demolished and a new temple to Rama be built in its place.

As Lal's earlier excavations of the site had provided no evidence to support the temple claims, the VHP archaeologists proceeded to manufacture it. Suddenly, in a right-wing Hindu magazine, Lal remembered having discovered what he considered to be burnt brick pillar bases during the excavations, though he had not considered this worth publishing at the time. These were now taken as evidence that a columned temple had once stood on the site. Later independent analysis of photographs of the trench in which Lal claimed to have found the pillar bases found that they were actually the remains of various walls of different, non-contemporaneous structural phases, and could not have been load-bearing structures (Mandal 2003). Despite this, Lal had made the following statement at a conference in 1988:

> It is abundantly clear there did exist a twelfth-century temple at the site, which was destroyed and some parts incorporated in the body of the Babri Masjid. (Lal 2001, p. 119)

Despite his adamant position, other than one photograph, Lal has never made the notebooks and sketches of his excavation available to other scholars so that his interpretation could be tested (Sharma 2001, p. 132), and has not come forward and testified in court at any point. Instead, he later wrote that the evidence was 'so eloquent that no further comments are necessary' (Lal 2008, p. 68). It is difficult to accept Lal's explanation of events and not come to the conclusion that the structural elements he had previously thought insignificant suddenly became temple foundations only in order to manufacture support for the nationalists' cause.

By 1990 the situation had become so hotly contested that the national government set up a commission of enquiry to determine once and for all whether a Hindu temple had ever been demolished in Ayodhya to build the mosque. To answer this question authoritatively, a subcommittee was formed of historians and archaeologists, half nominated by the VHP and half by the Muslim Babri Masjid Action Committee or BMAC (Rao 2006, p. 82).

In February 1992 the BJP decided that it had waited long enough, and by including the rebuilding of the supposed Hindu temple in its election manifesto, and with a BJP government now also in control of Uttar Pradesh, the fate of the Babri Masjid was effectively sealed. By July 1991 land had been acquired around the mosque, and preparation of the surrounding area for construction began. In June of 1992, these levelling activities led to the discovery by VHP workmen of a large pit filled with stone sculptures three metres below the surface, which were claimed to have come from a Hindu temple (Sharma *et al.* 1992, p. 1), and an area of walls and brick floors, claimed to be from a very large structure pre-dating Islamic occupation, which had clearly been demolished (Sharma *et al.* 1992, p. 11), almost too perfectly proving the temple destruction theory. The big problem with these new discoveries was that they were not excavated by archaeologists, so their stratigraphic and cultural contexts were not recorded, they were never properly documented and many of the objects have never actually been seen by anyone else. Independently analysing the information available on the stone sculptures, Mandal concluded that they could not be dated to the period of the postulated temple because their stratigraphic locations were not recorded, and the wide range of weathering patterns on the various objects indicated that they actually came from a range of locations and periods (Mandal 2003, p. 45).

The final meeting of VHP and BMAC historians and archaeologists took place on 5 December 1992. Against a background of over 100,000 VHP *kar sevaks* (holy volunteers) converging on Ayodhya, BMAC protested that this made the meeting pointless, and it broke up because relations between the two sides had become too hostile (Rao 2006, p. 99). On 6 December the *kar sevaks*, ignoring security forces, stormed the Masjid and within hours it had been totally demolished and Hindu idols were placed on the site (Rao 2006, p. 156), an event that sparked off communal violence in which over 2,000 people were killed.

In the days following the demolition, the national press reported that large stone objects and other remains indicative of a Hindu temple had been recovered from below the mosque, as though these were archaeological fact. As Ratnagar has commented (2003, p. 70): '...they have gone so far as to claim that an act of mob violence and the destruction of a five-century old structure amount to a valid retrieval of archaeological evidence!'

In 2002, the ASI was instructed by a High Court order to investigate the site once more, in order to definitively answer the question of whether a temple had once been demolished below the mosque. The site was then excavated by the ASI over a six-month period in 2003. Independent observers of the excavations reported that correct archaeological standards and procedures were not followed (Mandal and Ratnagar 2007, p. 29). In the end, the report concluded only that a 'huge structure' had been located, which had been dated to the eleventh–twelfth century, and indirectly insinuated that this was a temple. Once again, independent analysis of the excavation report and methods concluded that there was no logic in this conclusion, and that there was no evidence of demolition in the sixteenth century, 'but of vandalism in the twentieth century' (Mandal and Ratnagar 2007, pp. 129–131). Essentially, the ASI report was seen as a whitewash aimed at supporting Hindutva claims behind a pretence of scientific objectivity: 'The rhetoric of finding proof through archaeology offers means of foreclosing dissent by invoking the authority of performing "science"' (Guha 2005, p. 422). By allowing events to get to the stage where the mosque was destroyed, and then by allowing the ASI to produce a heavily biased report, the Indian government clearly no longer stood so firmly behind Nehru's 'secular and non-communal ideal'.

Because events surrounding the Ayodhya demolition were so explosive and had so much news coverage, outside of India one could be forgiven for believing it to be a unique, if disturbing, occurrence. This is not the case however, and other Indian heritage sites have in turn become the targets of right-wing nationalism, following the lead of events in Ayodhya.

POLITICAL CULTURE, SOFT INTERVENTIONS AND NATION BUILDING

Since its founding in 1964, the VHP had created a long list of sites (mostly mosques) in India that they believed had either been built over Hindu temples (Brass 1995, p. 241), or were offensive to Hindus in some other way. Hindu nationalists also worked to prepare the public by deliberately misrepresenting the number of cases where Hindu temples had been destroyed in order for mosques to be built in the past. B.B. Lal has written of 'hundreds of examples, all over the country' (Lal 2008, p. 66), while Goel lists over 2,000 Muslim monuments that he claims 'stand on the site and/or are built from materials of deliberately demolished Hindu temples' (Goel 1990, p. 62), as a result of 'large scale destruction' by 'Islamised invaders' (Goel 1990, p. vii). The numbers have been further inflated to 30,000 temples in the political rhetoric of VHP leader Pravin Togadia (Mahaprashasta 2009). These assertations have been refuted by Eaton, who shows that temple destruction was very seldom for religious purposes but was rather a facet of statebuilding, whereby it was part of the process of erasing the authority of a defeated Hindu ruler, and was also practiced in Hindu–Hindu conflict (Eaton 2000, pp. 104–107). He is only able to identify 80 known cases of temple desecration between 1192 and 1760 (Eaton 2000, pp. 128–131).

This is essentially a process of deliberately planting fake historical facts and memories in the minds of the public, and unfortunately the Hindutva message has been repeated much more frequently than it has been refuted in the media. A result of this is that many *kar sevaks* have pledged to reclaim thousands of sites (Bayley 1993, p. 12); all that is needed is for the right degree of communal tension to exist and any of the sites on the VHP list could fall victim.

This is what happened in Gujarat on 27 February 2002 when a large group of VHP *kar sevaks* were returning by train from Ayodhya where they had been continuing to agitate for a temple to be built on the now levelled site. There had been a series of communal clashes between the *kar sevaks* and Muslims as they travelled through the town of Godhra, and a rumour spread that they had kidnapped two Muslim women, causing the emergency brake on the train to be pulled. A mob of angry Muslims attacked the carriage that the activists were riding in and it was set alight—within an hour 59 people from the train were dead (Swami 2002). Over the next month, communal violence flared in the state, with an official death toll of 850, unofficially estimated to be as high as 2000 (Human Rights Watch 2002, p. 4).

During this period of communal violence religious and cultural heritage sites were also systematically targeted, with 298 dargahs, 205 mosques, 17 temples and three churches being either damaged or destroyed within two months (Pandey 2002). This was a carefully planned and well-resourced operation:

> The famous 500-year-old masjid in Isanpur, which was an ASI monument, was destroyed with the help of cranes and bulldozers. The famous Urdu Poet Wali Gujarati's dargah was also razed to the ground at Shahibaug in Ahmedabad. While a hanuman [a Hindu god] shrine was built over its debris initially, all that was removed overnight and the plot was [paved] and merged with the adjoining road. (Chenoy *et al.* 2002)

POLITICAL CULTURE, SOFT INTERVENTIONS AND NATION BUILDING

These are not the only nationalist events related to heritage that have occurred in Gujarat since Ayodhya. The state has had a BJP government since 1995, and the Chief Minister, Narendra Modi, is notorious for stirring up communal conflict. In such a climate, right-wing nationalism continues to be directed at heritage, with even an important World Heritage Site under threat. Located in ever-volatile Godhra, Champaner-Pavagadh Archaeological Park received World Heritage status in 2004. An important aspect of the site is that it contains a mixture of Hindu and Muslim elements, and as an early Islamic, pre-Mughal city it exhibits a unique blend and transition between the two traditions (UNESCO 2004, p. 28). Almost all of the Muslim families living at Champaner left following the 2002 riots (Sreenivas 2004), and the Gujarat government upset the Islamic Relief Committee in 2004 by producing brochures for the annual Navratri festival which listed all of the monuments in the park other than the Muslim shrines (Sreenivas 2004). The state government is attempting to promote the multicultural nature of the region in a belated attempt to look good despite its complicity in the 2002 riots, but such omissions still occur and, especially, syncretic places of worship are ignored, as these contradict the Hindutva notion of a natural state of conflict between the religions. The situation has also been greatly exacerbated by a local BJP politician. Complaining that the site showcases more Muslim monuments than Hindu ones, and leveraging community dissatisfaction with building restrictions, he has begun agitating to have World Heritage status removed from the site (Khan 2007), a move that is feared would lead to a loss of protection for the site, and the eventual destruction of the Muslim sections of it (Abdi 2007). At the same time, in nearby Vadodara the authorities have recently displayed open disregard for Muslim heritage during road construction by destroying part of a medieval Muslim graveyard containing the grave of a prominent Sufi, on the grounds that it was 'encroaching on public land' (Westcoat 2007, p. 59).

Even highly prominent politicians in Gujarat have been active in asserting a Hindu ownership of the past. For example, in 2003, while he was state Minister for Science and Technology, Murli Manohar Joshi claimed evidence of a 9,500-year-old Hindu civilization had been discovered in the Gulf of Cambay (Venkatesh and Radhakrishna 2003). So far his discovery has only received support from Graham Hancock and received no further attention, but it demonstrates the nationalist leaning of Modi's government.

Karnataka is another state in which the methods of leveraging heritage as a communal issue used at Ayodhya have been redeployed. In this case, a Sufi shrine in the Western Ghats, the Guru Dattatreya Baba Budangiri Swamy dargah, is already being compared to the Babri Masjid in the media. Although controlled by Muslims, the shrine is syncretic in nature and is also used by Hindu worshippers of an incarnation of Shiva known as Dattatreya who have been peaceably allowed joint access to the shrine for their rituals for centuries. The VHP has been campaigning to 'liberate' the shrine for several years, and in 2003 the BJP ominously became involved, with local party leaders going so far as to publicly

POLITICAL CULTURE, SOFT INTERVENTIONS AND NATION BUILDING

state that they intended to turn the issue into 'another Ayodhya', and vowing to 'repeat Gujarat' (Srikanth 2003).

The strategy employed at Ayodhya has been carefully replicated here, with Hindutva propaganda attempting to win over the media and popular opinion. As in Ayodhya, where the Babri Masjid came to be known more popularly as 'Ramjanambhoomi', so the shrine's historical Muslim name of 'Bababudangiri' is being replaced with the Hindu 'Dattareya Peeta' (Taneja 2006). In order to further stoke local tensions, *kar sevaks* have been brought in from across the country for rallies, with one annually timed to coincide provocatively with the 6 December demolition of the Babri Masjid (Srikanth 2003). The political nature of the movement is more than apparent in the way that things flare up most in the run-up to elections, and while Karnataka is currently between these things seem relatively quiet. Many expect things to come to a head eventually though: 'The silence is eerie, however, and with a BJP government in power, pregnant' (Srinivasaraju 2009). The first signs of this happening may be recent moves by the BJP to renovate the site according to Hindu requirements, in full contravention of a Supreme Court order (Sayeed 2009).

Activists in Maharashtra have also sought to follow the Ayodhya model, as during the lead up to an election campaign in the town of Pratapgarh in 2004. Targeting the tomb of the seventeenth-century Muslim general Afzal Khan, the VHP organized a protest against buildings being built around the site by the Muslim charitable trust that manages the site. With *kar sevaks* brought in from other areas, around 1,200 protesters marched towards the site, encouraged by inflammatory rhetoric, with one local BJP leader for example being quoted as saying '... Why is the government supporting a trust which looks after an enemy's tomb?' (Katakam 2004). The protest turned violent when finally stopped by police and in the end 250 people were arrested. While the official aim was to remove 'illegal' structures around the tomb, there can be little doubt as to what would have happened without police intervention, as stated by one VHP member: '... We would have done it with our own hands, like Babri Masjid, what did we have then in our hands?' (Menon 2004).

Despite the fact that the above events in Gujarat, Karnataka and Maharashtra all represent a clear continuation of Hindutva tactics deployed in Ayodhya, it has in recent years become common to hear that the right-wing threat posed by the BJP and Hindutva has been greatly lessened for the foreseeable future. This is largely based on the fact that, once in power, the BJP adopted more centrist policies, for example by withdrawing its calls for the building of a temple at Ayodhya. The fact that it then also lost the federal elections in 2004 was seen as demonstrating a change of heart by the electorate following the Gujarat riots, which would force the party to maintain a more moderate stance if it were to stand a chance of re-election in the future. All indicators, however, point towards this move to the centre as being a matter of temporary expediency only, and that in fact the right-wing agenda is still being pursued with determination and mounting momentum.

The issues which led to the BJP being voted out of power have not been resolved by that action. Most obviously, those responsible for the destruction of the Babri Masjid, for the ensuing violence and for the later Gujarat riots have never been brought to justice, and there are thus large numbers of right-wing sympathizers who know through experience that they can take the law into their own hands without the threat of punishment, and can be called upon again in future. The real effects of the BJP's time in power can be expected to continue for a long time to come, as during this period the influence of Hindutva became deeply embedded in many state institutions. Thus, while the BJP itself appears on the back foot, the RSS itself has actually been expanding due to this foundation (*Times of India* 2009a). The continued trajectory of the Sang Parivar has been demonstrated by elements within it being linked to recent terrorist attacks, such as those in Goa in 2009.

In the meantime, Hindutva politics, currently deemed inexpedient for the BJP, are being expressed outside of it. For example, the former Chief Minister of Uttar Pradesh, Kalyan Singh (who was head of the state government when the Ayodhya demolition took place), has recently started his own right-wing party, 'that will espouse the ideology of Hindutva, cultural nationalism, social justice, social harmony and development' (*Indian Express* 2009). The BJP itself has in turn continued to stir communal tensions when absolutely necessary to keep things on track, such as by briefly promoting the Ayodhya temple project in the hopes of influencing the recent Allahabad High Court verdict.

The greatest evidence that the ideology of Hindutva has become internalized by the state is the way that the Ayodhya case has been handled. Determining final responsibility for the events at Ayodhya was assigned to a commission, which then took 17 years (including 48 extensions) to produce a report that was finally submitted to the government in June of 2009 (*Times of India* 2009b). This was followed by a judgement of the Allahabad High Court in September of 2010, which determined that the site should be divided into three parts among Hindus, the Nirmohl Akhara Hindu sect and Muslims. The judges accepted the ASI report, completely ignoring all evidence to the contrary that had been submitted by independent parties:

> The disputed structure was constructed on the site of the old structure after demolition of the same. The Archaeological Survey of India has proved that the structure was a massive Hindu religious structure. (Sharma 2010)

They also accepted the Hindutva view that the site is the birthplace of Ram:

> The area covered under the central dome of the disputed structure is the birthplace of Lord Rama as per faith and belief of Hindus. (Agarwal 2010)

While the above ruling is certain to be taken to the Supreme Court by one or more of the parties, it is already certain to have wide-reaching consequences. Writing in 2003, Kesavan predicted that were such a verdict to be delivered, then 'imperceptibly, India would become another country' (Kesavan 2003, p. 67), and this may turn out to be an understatement. A legal precedent has now been set by which the religious beliefs of one community have been seen as sufficient in order to claim land from another group. The result of this will surely be a massive increase in the number of claims being made by Hindu groups throughout India. It will also greatly embolden Hindu nationalists overall, as was shown by immediate demands being made by the BJP that the Muslims relinquish their one-third share of the Ayodhya site.

In parallel to these events at major sites, the philosophy of Hindutva has also been systematically promoted within academia, with many scholars advancing nationalist theories arguing for indigenous origins of Hindu culture. At the centre of these theories is the Aryan race issue, where it is not so much the case that '... nothing less than the origin of Indian civilization is at stake' (Danino 2003, p. 21), but that nothing less than the ownership of Indian civilization is. The idea of an 'Aryan' heritage in India goes back to the research of Max Müller, who had proposed a homeland in Central Asia for the Aryans, who then spread to Europe and South Asia in two separate migrations, and introduced Vedic or Hindu culture to India (Müller 1883). In part, this theory has a strong attraction for Hindu nationalists, as claiming Hindu and Aryan culture to be the same thing effectively separates Hindus from all other people in India. The idea that the Aryans were invaders however is strongly refuted, as this would reduce the strength of claims to indigeneity, placing Hindus in the same category as Muslims and Christians as immigrants. The preferred version of the Aryan theory improves Hindu self-esteem and legitimizes the social status of upper-caste Hindus, and it also installs Hindus as 'the inheritors of the land since the beginning of History' (Thapar 2000, p. 15), and all others as alien. At the extreme, in the same way that Nazi treatment of the Jews was 'theoretically excused' through creating the distinction of Aryans and Semites, so now the mistreatment and exclusion of other groups in India—e.g. Muslims, Sikhs, Christians and tribal peoples—is also excused (Thapar 1996, p. 10).

One strategy employed in establishing this position is to identify Hindus with the earliest known advanced culture in India, the Indus civilization, which is best known for the sites of Harappa and Mohenjo-daro. By claiming continuity of a Vedic culture from the Indus civilization to modern Hinduism, essentially a 'foundational myth' (Guha 2005, p. 418), any share of this prestige is denied to other groups in India. Archaeologists have become involved in this in a number of ways. Often this involves making a wide range of comparisons of what is known of Indus culture to aspects of modern Hindu culture, seeking similarities such as methods of farming, arts and crafts and household items, and using examples from vastly different geographical locations and timescales to make arguments which are both tenuous yet at the same time difficult to refute (Guha 2005, p. 415). The theories ignore the fact that even without full continuity these aspects of culture are naturally diffusive and would have been picked up by neighbouring groups through trade and intermingling anyway. The fact that many of the tribal cultures in India as well as those of neighbouring regions seem to

POLITICAL CULTURE, SOFT INTERVENTIONS AND NATION BUILDING

have retained aspects of Indus-like material culture with greater fidelity is conveniently ignored (Thapar 1996, p. 21).

Many methods have been used in attempts to prove the Vedic character of the Indus civilization. These have included attempting to demonstrate the presence of horses in the latter by Jha and Rajaram (2000), later demonstrated to have been achieved through computer manipulation of images on Indus seals (Witzel and Farmer 2000, p. 6). Well over a thousand publications on the Indus symbols have been published (Possehl 1996, p. 76), along with over 50 decipherment attempts (Misra 1992, p. 12), most of which aim to prove that the symbols represent Sanskrit language. This is despite solid linguistic and archaeological work demonstrating late Vedic did not appear until two millennia after the height of the Indus civilization, and that the symbol system is more likely 'a relatively simple system of religious-political signs that could be reinterpreted in any language' (Farmer *et al.* 2004, p. 45). B.B. Lal has in turn tried to make up for the lack of physical evidence for written language by arguing that two small pieces of terracotta with no markings on them are highly likely to be writing tablets, based on a comparison with the wooden *takhıs* used until recently in Indian schools (Lal 2002, p. 135).

Hindutva scholars have also aimed to prove that the Saraswati river, mentioned throughout the Rigveda, was in fact located in India., with B.B. Lal making the case, based on two verses of the epic poem, that it must actually have flowed through India and right past the famous Indus civilization site of Mohenjo-daro on its way out to the Arabian Sea (Lal 2002, p. 15). Once again Lal is willing to overstate the importance of weak evidence, in this case by claiming that the Rigveda is a source of incontrovertible evidence, and he defends the position by labelling any who disagree as (anti-Hindu) bigots: '**Can we afford to ignore the categorical evidence provided by these two adjacent verses? Surely not, unless we blindfold ourselves under a spell of bigotry**' (Lal 2002, p. 11; the bold type is Lal's). The theory nevertheless gained official sanction under a BJP-led government in 2003 with the creation of the Saraswati Heritage Project, which was given a huge budget and placed under the ASI (Guha 2005, p. 418). However, once the BJP was out of power the new government carried out a review of the ASI's work, and in 2006 the Parliamentary Standing Committee on Transport, Tourism and Culture reported that the ASI had failed to follow correct processes in choosing sites for excavation. Pointing out that the project was extremely pro-Hindu, they stated regret that so many resources had so far been used '. . . just to excavate a mythological river whereas, several other monuments/heritage sites of national importance are languishing due to acute shortage of funds', and the budget for the project was subsequently slashed (Chhibber 2006). Similarly to many commentators on Ayodhya, the committee expressed serious concern that right-wing considerations had led members of the ASI to compromise the scientific integrity of the project:

> The ASI is the custodian of the rich cultural heritage and as such its role to safeguard the cultural fabric of the country is of crucial national importance.

POLITICAL CULTURE, SOFT INTERVENTIONS AND NATION BUILDING

> Therefore, the committee reiterates that before undertaking any excavation of any such mythological projects like the Saraswati Heritage Project, the ASI should make proper scientific and technical appraisal and no extraneous factors should go into the decision-making. (Chhibber 2006)

Tellingly, the number of works thus seeking to prove an indigenous origin for Hindu culture has grown in parallel to the BJP and the Ayodhya movement, openly seeking to reinforce a popular political paradigm, rather than through any direct relation to newly discovered evidence.

In addition to the academic world, the Hindutva perspective is also being pushed within the Indian education system. While the BJP was in power between 1998 and 2004, the National Council of Educational Research and Training (NCERT) produced new history textbooks for schools that contained 'appropriate rewritings', and deleted many sections from earlier ones. Similarly, the Indian Council of Historical Research (ICHR) was 'overhauled' and given a new agenda and staff in line with nationalist priorities (Sen 2005, p. 63). A major aspect of this was once again the focus on Hindu cultural continuity—the Indus civilization was renamed the 'Indus-Saraswati Civilization' in textbooks, and developments in mathematics, philosophy and science were given much earlier, Vedic origins:

> Such untruths have been the staple diet upon which the cadre of the Sangh Parivar has been brought up. But then, to introduce such false statements into the school curriculum is indeed a dangerous proposition. The havoc that indifferent scholarship combining with a distorting ideology could cause in school education is all too apparent. (*The Hindu* 2002)

Most of these changes were reversed when the BJP lost its majority in the national elections, and the new NCERT textbooks have for the most part been highly regarded. There have been some cases where the same issues continue however, such as the class 11 textbook *Ancient India* by Makkhan Lal, which still contained over 137 historically incorrect assertions and errors (Habib *et al.* 2003, pp. 27–57). The Hindu bias in the curriculum also continues in BJP-ruled states such as Himachal Pradesh, where, for example, a chapter on the Muslim painter M.F. Husain (who had controversially portrayed Hindu goddesses in the nude) has been removed from textbooks (Phull 2010).

When Hindu nationalist content was removed from the national school programme, other ways to influence children's education were sought. For example, the BJP had increased the amount of Sanskrit and Vedic literature taught in schools, which was then reduced again once they lost power in favour of a more multicultural curriculum. The response of Hindutva was to establish Sanskrit summer camps. In a *Washington Post* article, an interview with a 19-year-old camp attendee confirmed the success of the scheme: '... when I study Sanskrit, I learn who I am. It is my identity' (Lakshmi 2008).

The aim of shaping education to conform to Hindutva ideology is not being limited to India. During a review of textbooks to be used in Californian sixth grade classes in 2006, several US organizations, including the Hindu Education Foundation, demanded changes to sections of the textbooks that did not show Hinduism in a positive light, or that discussed theories of an Aryan migration into India rather than cultural continuity of Vedic culture (Baldauf 2006). The situation went to court, with the Hindutva claims eventually being thrown out in June of 2009 (Walsh 2009). Several expatriate organizations have also become extremely vigilant in defending conservative Hindu interests in the United Kingdom. M.F. Hussain was again the target when the two groups known as the Hindu Forum of Britiain and Hindu Human Rights forced an exhibition of his works in London to close in 2006, with protests that threatened to turn violent. This followed a 2005 campaign that forced the Royal Mail to withdraw a Christmas stamp featuring a Hindu family, which was claimed to be culturally insensitive (Zavos 2008).

As can be seen from the examples listed above, an overall aim of Hindu nationalism is to create a large body of literature that emphasizes the continuity of Hindu culture in India from the earliest times, and denigrates the contribution of other cultures. It is as if once this body of work is in place, it will be possible to simply ignore the work and claims to the contrary of mainstream heritage academics. This is something that Possehl (1996, p. 168) has noted in regard to decipherment research on the Indus symbol system, where while not all, but much of the work is following a nationalist agenda: '...researchers barrel ahead in their own directions, showing little evidence that they can, or even care to, draw on the work of their colleagues'. Thapar (2000, p. 16) has commented on the same thing: 'Dogmatic assertions with no space for alternative ideas often arise from a sense of inferiority and the fear of debate. Hence the determination to prevent the publication of volumes on history which do not conform to Hindutva ideology.' Often researchers who work within frameworks and models that are established within their disciplines, and with the consensus of international colleagues, are described as neo-colonialists, elitists, hypocrites, right-wing Christians, bigots and extremists, without seriously attempting to rebut their academic arguments. This can also turn violent, as in January of 2004 when protests against a book by US academic James Laine on the eighteenth-century Hindu ruler Shivaji ended with the storming of the Bhandarkar Oriental Research Institute in Pune. Hindu activists ransacked the archives, destroying and damaging hundreds of rare manuscripts in retaliation for the institute having allowed Laine to conduct research there, forcing Oxford University Press to withdraw the book from the Indian market (Suroor 2004) and the Maharashtra state government to ban it completely, until the Supreme Court finally lifted the ban in 2010 (*Times of India* 2010).

There is considerable concern within mainstream Indian archaeology about the activities of these fringe nationalist researchers, who often come from unrelated backgrounds and yet publish prolifically on archaeological and historical 'facts' that back up Hindu nationalist agendas. This was summarized by D.P. Agarwal in his address to a major Indian archaeology conference at the start of the new millennium:

POLITICAL CULTURE, SOFT INTERVENTIONS AND NATION BUILDING

> I would like to express my fears about the neophyte archaeologists. With these newly converted friends of Indian archaeology, it does not need any enemies. Their over-zealous but misinformed efforts are not only befuddling the issues, but are diverting the efforts in the wrong directions. (Agarwal 2000, p. 15)

Discussing the divisions in the discipline over Ayodhya, Paddayya highlights one possible outcome of this problem:

> India's past and its students, instead of serving as a source of enlightenment for society, have become a burden on it. It is not unreasonable that the ordinary citizen has now started expressing doubts about the relevance of both to society. (Paddayya 1995, p. 141)

While many do not believe that archaeology, history and the sciences can ever offset the 'irrational anger' and 'wrath of the people' when stirred by communal politics as in the case of Ayodhya (Rao 1994, p. 161), the potential of the situation to seriously escalate should not be forgotten. This was well described by Kymlicka in *Multicultural Citizenship*:

> ... the fear is that group-differentiated rights will undermine the sense of shared civic identity that holds a liberal society together. These rights will be a source of disunity that could lead to the dissolution of the country, or, less drastically, to a reduced willingness to make the mutual sacrifices and accommodations necessary for a functioning democracy. (Kymlicka 1995, p. 173)

This is the ultimate danger posed by the Hindutva movement and its attempts to appropriate the Indian past, that in their attempts to create a unified Hindu nation-state, they may in fact eventually bring about the collapse of an already fragile and fractious arrangement.

Both local and international heritage academics have not only the ability but also a vital responsibility to redress the misrepresentation of the past for political means in India. Research carried out with the aim of gaining a clear understanding of the highly diverse and interwoven roles that all groups living in South Asia have played as part of their common history has the potential to offset right-wing nationalist misinformation, and to assist in creating a higher level of cohesion between the various national minorities of the Indian nation-state. There are many areas in which there is great potential for this to be achieved.

The prehistory of South Asia is as yet relatively poorly understood compared to other parts of the world (Chakrabarti 2006, p. 474). By filling in the details, archaeologists have the opportunity to emphasize what is (at least until now) uncontestedly common to the heritage of everyone in the region, and to uncover the important role that it has played alongside neighbouring regions in the history of humankind overall. The potential for the study of Middle Pleistocene hominins is greater in India than anywhere else in the Old World (Dennel 2009, p. 336), and research into the Siwalik region as a possible migratory corridor for *Homo erectus* could provide pivotal evidence regarding the competing 'Out of Africa' and multiregional development models in human evolutionary studies (Chakrabarti

POLITICAL CULTURE, SOFT INTERVENTIONS AND NATION BUILDING

2006, p. 477). India also offers an ability to look more deeply into prehistory than many other regions. The site of Bhimbetka in Madhya Pradesh, for example, possesses petroglyphs dating back three times further than any discovered elsewhere in the world (Chakrabarti 2006, p. 478), and this uniqueness combined with a rich ethnographic record of hunter gatherer societies (Dennel 2009, p. 336) means that there is enormous potential to gain much greater insight into human societies from the paleolithic onwards. In the words of Kennedy, a long-term researcher in South Asian paleoanthropology: '... we are at the threshold of an exciting era in the history of science as India takes its rightful place in our understanding of human evolution' (Kennedy 2005, p. 40).

As can be seen from the section earlier in this article, the way in which evidence of the Indus civilization is interpreted is key to whether it can be co-opted by the Hindu right. While it is going to be extremely important to continue rebutting unfounded claims made by right-wing researchers, it will also be crucial to continue with investigations that unravel the true nature of this ancient culture. Intriguingly, there are indications from current research that the Indus civilization, covering an enormous geographic area, may actually have incorpo-rated multiple national minorities and languages, and yet still managed to maintain its unity and cohesiveness over a very long period of time (Farmer *et al.* 2004, pp. 44–45). The potential contributions of this to building a modern Indian national identity based on unity in diversity are obvious. Taking a more multidisciplinary approach to Indus research would not only greatly increase the range of information available to answer the larger questions (Shinde *et al.* 2006, p. 71), but it would also help to refute the claims of some right-wing nationalist researchers that the archaeological approach is too narrow and dogmatic.

It is also important that the syncretic history of many Indian sites be brought to the attention of students and the public, emphasizing the fact that Hinduism, Islam and other religions have not only existed peacefully together but have even shared their very places of worship, completely in opposition to the concept of periods of singular usage broken by violent transitions promoted by Hindutva. This is not only essential for well-known sites such as Sri Guru Dattatreya Bababudan Swamy Dargah, Champaner and the Babri Masjid, but the simple fact that India has a very large number of syncretic shrines (Burman 1996) can help to counter the argument of intolerance and destruction. Where incorrect claims are made about historical temple desecration, these need to be systematically refuted.

There are also very many other sites of great importance in India across all ages, which need to be better publicized, preserved and managed. The early historic city of Sisupalgarh in Orissa is a good example of this, as it is an example of an as yet poorly understood culture that possessed a high level of social organization and economic development (Mohanty and Smith 2008, p. 11). It is by excavating such sites that the diversity of India's common past comes to light, and they have the potential to take the public's interest because they are both monumental and accessible. An interview with the BBC illustrates this well, where after noting that it may have supported up to 25,000 inhabitants, the excavation co-leader was quoted as saying: 'The significance of this ancient city becomes clear when one bears in mind the fact that the population of classical Athens was barely 10,000' (Sahu 2008). By placing the magnitude of the Indian past into context, it should not be hard to encourage public interest in its richness and diversity. Unfortunately, in this case due to a lack of funds and a preference by the ASI to focus on other areas of Indian heritage, what would be the highly visible remains of a city that would qualify for World Heritage status are covered over at the end of each excavation season.

It is similarly important that regions of India that are currently under-studied in Indian archaeology receive more attention. Often these areas share borders with other countries and are more culturally varied, so they can add a lot to knowledge of migration, trade and diversity. Examples are the Assam region in the north-east, with its proximity to South-East Asia (Hazarika 2006), and Jammu and Kashmir and Himalchal Pradesh in the north-west, close to Middle Asia where researchers '...expect an avalanche of new research to change our view of mankind's first attempt at civilisation' (Lawler 2007, p. 590). It is only by studying the migrations and interactions between the various regions that a complete picture of the past can be arrived at, in contrast to the more indigenous models favoured by Hindu nationalists. Ratnagar (2004) has also stressed that elements of cultural anthropology and ethnic archaeology are missing from courses offered in Indian archaeology departments, something which would better equip students for understanding ancient and non-Hindu sites, while Bernbeck and Pollock (1996, p. S141) have argued that it is important to demonstrate the way that both membership of communities and their identities have changed over time, in order to refute the idea that they are unchanging and that it is possible to equate a modern population directly with a past one. New perspectives and methodologies are in fact developing within Indian archaeology and history that have the potential to subvert the dominant research paradigms and agendas. The employment of indigenous epistemological transitions has been urged (Paddayya 1995), and the rise of subaltern studies promises to be more inclusive of minorities and interpretations of their pasts. According to Prakash, discussing the journal of the same name, the '...critical force of Subaltern Studies lies in its disruption of such enduring colonialist and nationalist essentializations as the unitary Indic civilization and the nation' (Prakash 1992, p. 373).

Finally and most importantly, archaeologists and historians need to become as actively involved in education as possible, both of schoolchildren and the public. Not only do they need to work hard to combat the attempts at misinformation from right-wing nationalists, they also need to try to improve public knowledge of the past, as well as their understanding of how archaeology, history and science work, so that they can judge the information being presented to them in the media. There are excellent programmes already underway in this regard, such as that run by the Sharma Children's Museum near Chennai, which teaches children 'introductory archaeology, associated sciences and ethnoarchaeology, the story of human evolution, cultural phases in India from the Palaeolithic to the Iron Age' as well as the archaeology of the local region (Pappu 2000, p. 485). Equipped with knowledge such as this, as opposed to that which is learnt in the Hindutva-organized Sanskrit camps, these children can face the future with both an appreciation for the diversity of their own country, and an objective toolkit for interpreting issues of identity and communalism. This is extremely encouraging, and is exactly the kind of development that Paddayya has stressed as most necessary in reference to the 1992 events at Ayodhya:

> ...a more mature response requires that, instead of bewailing this legacy of British scholarship, Indians take concrete steps to educate society about the past. Precious little has been done over the last forty-five years. The result is the indiscriminate use of the past by interested groups for their own ends...A non-partisan understanding of the past on the part of the ordinary citizen, and his/her ability to appreciate the universality of human culture...are the best insurance against any abuse of the past. (Paddayya 1995, pp. 141–142)

This has also been identified by Sen as being the single most important way to counter Hindutva:

> The deepest weakness of contemporary Hindu politics lies, however, in its reliance on ignorance at different levels—from exploiting credulity in order to promote militant obscurantism to misrepresenting India's past in order to foster factional nationalism and communal fascism. The weakest link in the sectarian chain is this basic dependence on both simple and sophisticated ignorance. That is where a confrontation is particularly overdue. (Sen 1993, p. 22)

Consequences and Conclusion

The potential consequences of a continued rise of the Hindu right in India, with a parallel leveraging of heritage to create identity based conflicts, should not be underestimated, and archaeologists and historians can play a vital role by nullifying this strategy. Following the Allahabad High Court verdict in favour of the nationalists, a proliferation of demands that heritage sites all over India be turned over to Hindu control can be expected, but as in the cases outlined in this article, the human cost of the decision is not yet known.

While Hindu nationalism seeks to portray India as culturally homogenous, it is at the same time highly divisive. It is possible that it could over time lead to an India so fractured that the state would no longer be able sustain the process of governing described by Arendt, and would either have to concede a greater political role to more minorities, removing them from their stateless condition and facing ever greater challenges in governing, or be faced with secession movements in which they remove themselves. Greater autonomy for any of these groups is likely in turn to lead to increased calls for a separate Hindu state. An alternative would be, in opposition to Hindu nationalism, to take a non-sectarian approach to nation-building with an emphasis on common strands of identity that would encourage minorities to remain within the state. In both cases, as seen in the preceding sections, the use of heritage plays a highly significant role.

One year before the Babri Masjid demolition, Brass described both India and the USSR as '...confronted by crises of national unity, including the expression of explicit secessionist demands from several ethnic and nationality groups...' (Brass 1991, p. 301). The USSR collapsed later that year, and since then it can be argued that the continuing rise of right-wing nationalism in India has led to even greater internal turmoil and instability. As a coherent opposition to Hindu nationalism is yet to materialize and present an alternative identity and a vision of an inclusive identity, this can be expected to continue.

According to Singh, the first half of the twenty-first century is likely to see India facing major difficulties due to a necessary reorganization of its federal structure. This is in part due to significant changes in population distribution, where some states are coming to have very large populations but proportionally fewer seats in parliament, and because of concerns about the financial and administrative viability of some recently created states, and also the continuing unresolved special status of both Kashmir and Nagaland. This is seen as necessary, as the alternative of '...endless fragmentation of the Indian nation-state is not a solution but part of the problem of ungovernability and international instability' (Singh 2007, pp. 246–247). In order to mitigate the risks involved in this challenge, India will need to work to avoid the alienation of minorities by addressing their concerns and attempting to establish a more inclusive national identity.

Moves towards regional autonomy or secession would have serious consequences for the entire South Asian region, especially as India is currently surrounded by politically unstable and authoritarian states. Any granting of autonomy in India could spark independence movements in neighbouring states as well, such as Bhutan and Nepal, which both have significant minority populations (Misra 2004), and change to the sovereignty of Kashmir would aggravate relations with Pakistan. Internal disorder would also make it difficult for India to respond to international conflict situations, as evidenced by its recent reluctance to aid Sri Lanka in 2000 when its forces were already stretched with dealing with problems in Kashmir and its north-east states (Devotta 2003).

India's relations with both of its Muslim neighbours, Pakistan and Bangladesh, are currently highly strained, and there is a danger that a Hindu nationalist government pursuing anti-Muslim policies would cause these relations to deteriorate still further. Pakistan is widely seen as the largest threat to security in the region, both due to its support for militant Islam and its internal fragility, compounded by the fact that it is a nuclear power (Vicziany and Weigold 2003, p. 81). Should India not work towards lessening tensions and increasing trust this situation is not likely to improve, especially as both India and Pakistan are likely to come into conflict over developing interests in Central Asia, which are already leading them into an increasingly long-term and aggressively competitive involvement in Afghanistan (Pant 2010). The internal stability of Pakistan would also be impacted, as increased Hindu nationalism in India is likely to encourage both an increase in militancy among civilian groups and the strengthening of the position of the military itself, which has hardly proven itself a factor in promoting stable democracy. In a situation of decreased trust, the consequences of another 'strategic surprise' such as the 2008 attacks on Mumbai could be much more severe.

There is also the danger that, as has occurred in other countries, a nationalist government in India might adopt an expansionist agenda. The 'India Shining' campaign of 2004 clearly indicated the BJP's desire to both ally itself with business and to project a more powerful international identity (Wyatt 2005). Hindu nationalism has a history of international ambition that began with the Greater India Society, founded in Calcutta in the 1920s, and sought to demonstrate that Hindu civilization had both greatly influenced and to a degree colonized other parts of Asia. This included cultural claims to a wide swathe of territory, from Central Asia to the Pacific, including Tibet, Cambodia, Singapore, Burma, Java, Bali, Vietnam, Ceylon and even Japan (Bayley 2004, p. 713). Their work is now being picked up by Hindutva scholars, who lobby for increased engagement with these countries and those which have large immigrant Hindu populations such as Nepal, Malaysia, Indonesia and the Philippines (Mitra 2003, p. 411). According to Grant:

> Hindu nationalists view their nation as possessing the greatest claim to indigeneity for an area ... of the Earth's surface roughly equivalent to the official state claim of modern India. This includes the disputed areas of Kashmir, Ladakh, and Arunachal Pradesh. Nearby areas—including those claimed by Pakistan and Bangladesh (as well as perhaps Sri Lanka, Tibet and Nepal) are understood to be at their root part of this claim. (Grant 2005, p. 332)

As this article has argued, heritage is central to the pressing of this claim and it is clear that archaeologists and historians have a chance to play a very important role in determining the future of the Indian state, and of other states in the region. With Hindu nationalism posing a serious threat to stability and not showing signs of decline, it is vital to establish an effective opposition to it within these disciplines. This needs to not only include the production of well-balanced research, but must also carefully refute nationalist misinformation, and above all focus on public education. There is a tendency to underestimate the danger posed by the right, but it is only by determined and concerted action that this danger can be negated.

Acknowledgements

An outside perspective of the Indian situation, the views and any errors that this article contains are all my own. However, I would like to thank Harsh Kapoor Bisnupriya Basak, Gabriel Moshenska and the anonymous reviewers for their useful suggestions.

References

Abdi, R., 2007. BJP wants de-recognition of Champaner Word Heritage Site. *TwoCircles. net.* Available from: http://www.twocircles.net/2007oct23/bjp_wants_de_recognition_champaner_word_heritage_site.html [Accessed 4 July 2009].

Agarwal, D.P., 2001. The idea of India and its heritage: the millennial challenges. *Man and environment,* XXVI, 16–22.

Agarwal, S.A., Hon'ble, 2010. Decision of Hon'ble Special Full Bench hearing Ayodhya matters: gist of judgement. Allahabad High Court, 30 Sept. Available from: file:/// Users/brianhole/Desktop/AllahabadHC_300910_verdict/ayodhyafiles/hondvsj-gist-vol1. pdf [Accessed 1 October 2010].

Arendt, H., 1951. *The origins of totalitarianism.* San Diego, CA: Harcourt Brace & Company.

Arendt, H., 1958. *The human condition.* Chicago, IL: University of Chicago Press.

Baldauf, S., 2006. India history spat hits US. *Christian Science Monitor.* Available from: http://www.csmonitor.com/2006/0124/p01s03a-wosc.htm [Accessed 11 July 2009].

Bayley, S., 1993. History and the fundamentalists: India after the Ayodhya crisis. *Bulletin of the American Academy of Arts and Sciences,* 46 (7), 7–26.

Bayley, S., 2004. Imagining 'greater India': French and Indian visions of colonialism in the Indic mode. *Modern Asian studies,* 38 (3), 703–744.

Beales, D.E.D. and Biagni, E.F., 1971. *The risorgimento and the unification of Italy.* Sydney, Australia: George Allen & Unwin.

Bernbeck, R. and Pollock, S., 1996. Ayodhya, archaeology, and identity. *Current anthropology,* 37 (1), S138–S142.

Brass, P.R., 1991. *Ethnicity and nationalism: theory and comparison.* New Delhi: Sage Publications.

Brass, P.R., 1995. *The politics of India since independence.* Cambridge: Cambridge University Press.

Burman, J.J.R., 1996. Hindu-Muslim syncreticism in India. *Economic and political weekly,* 31 (20), 1211–1215.

Butler, J. and Spivak, G.C., 2007. *Who sings the nation-state? Language, politics, belonging.* Oxford: Seagull Books.

Chakrabarti, D.K., 2006. *The Oxford companion to Indian archaeology.* Oxford: Oxford University Press.

Chenoy, K.M., Nagar, V., Bose, P. and Krishnan, V., 2002. *Ethnic cleansing in Ahmedabad: a preliminary report.* Available from: http://www.revolutionarydemocracy.org/parl/ gujarat.htm [Accessed 9 July 2009].

Chhibber, M., 2006. Panel finds fault with Saraswati project. *The Tribune.* Available from: http://www.tribuneindia.com/2006/20061009/main2.htm [Accessed 12 July 2009].

Danino, M., 2003. The Harappan heritage and the Aryan problem. *Man and environment,* XXVIII, 21–32.

Dennel, R., 2009. *The Palaeolithic settlement of Asia.* Cambridge: Cambridge University Press.

Devotta, N., 2003. Is India over-extended? When domestic disorder precludes regional intervention. *Contemporary South Asia*, 12 (3), 365–380.

Eaton, R.M., 2000. *Essays on Islam and Indian history*. Oxford: Oxford University Press.

Farmer, S., Sproat, R. and Witzel, M., 2004. The collapse of the Indus-script thesis: the myth of a literate Harappan civilization. *Electronic journal of Vedic studies*, 11, 19–57.

Gillan, M., 2003. Bengal's past and present: Hindu nationalist contestations of history and regional identity. *Contemporary South Asia*, 12 (3), 381–398.

Goel, S.R., 1990. *Hindu temples: what happened to them?* New Delhi: Voice of India.

Gopal, S., Thapar, R., Chandra, B., Bhattacharya, S., Jaiswal, S., Mukhia, H., Panikkar, K.N., Champakalakshmi, R., Saberwal, S., Chattopadhyaya, B.D., Verma, R.N., Meenakshi, K., Alam, M., Singh, D., Mukherjee, M., Palat, M., Mukherjee, A., Ratnagar, S.F., Bhattacharya, N., Trivedi, K.K., Sharma, Y., Chakravarti, K., Josh, B., Gurukkal, R. and Ray, H., 1990. The political abuse of history: Babri Masjid-Rama Janmabhumi dispute. *Social scientist*, 18 (1–2), 76–81.

Grant, W.J., 2005. The space of the nation: an examination of the spatial productions of Hindu nationalism. *Nationalism and ethnic politics*, 11 (3), 321–347.

Guha, S., 2005. Negotiating evidence: history, archaeology and the Indus civilisation. *Modern Asian studies*, 39, 399–426.

Habib, I., Jaiswal, S. and Mukherjee, A., 2003. *History in the new NCERT text books for classes VI, IX and XI: a report and an index of errors*. Kolkata: Indian History Congress.

Hazarika, M., 2006. Neolithic culture of northeast India: a recent perspective on the origins of pottery and agriculture. *Ancient Asia*, 1, 25–43.

Human Rights Watch, 2002. We have no orders to save you. *State participation and complicity in communal violence in Gujarat*, 14 (3)(C).

Indian Express, 2009. A new political party of the Hindu right announced. *Indian Express*. Available from: http://communalism.blogspot.com/2009/12/new-political-party-of-hindu-right.html [Accessed 12 September 2010].

Jha, N. and Rajaram, N.S., 2000. *The deciphered Indus script: methodology, readings, interpretations*. Delhi: Aditya Prakashan.

Katakam, A., 2009. A tomb as target. *Frontline*, 21 (20). Available from: http://www.hinduonnet.com/fline/fl2120/stories/20041008006701100.htm [Accessed 17 September 2010].

Kennedy, K.A.R., 2005. Archaeological and anthropological research in South Asia: developments over the past fifty years. *Man and environment*, XXX, 36–41.

Kesavan, M., 2003. India's embattled secularism. *The Wilson quarterly*, 27 (1), 61–67.

Khan, A., 2007. Champaner-Pavagadh heritage tag runs into protests. Available from: http://www.indianexpress.com/story-print/215483/ [Accessed 9 July 2009].

Kulke, H. and Rothermund, D., 2004. *A history of India*. Abingdon: Routledge.

Kymlicka, W., 1995. *Multicultural citizenship*. Oxford: Clarendon Press.

Lakshmi, R., 2008. Summer camps revive India's ancient Sanskrit. *The Washington Post*. Available from: http://www.washingtonpost.com/wp-dyn/content/article/2008/06/14/AR2008061400892.html [Accessed 18 June 2008].

Lal, B.B., 1976–77. Excavation at Ayodhya, District Faizabad. *Indian archaeology—a review*, 52–53.

Lal, B.B., 2001. A note on the excavations at Ayodhya with reference to the Mandir-Masjid issue. *In*: R. Layton, P.G. Stone and J. Thomas, eds. *Destruction and conservation of cultural property*. London: Routledge, 117–126.

Lal, B.B., 2002. *The Sarasvati flows on: the continuity of Indian culture*. New Delhi: Aryan Books International.

Lal, B.B., 2008. *Rama: his historicity, Mandir and Setu*. New Delhi: Aryan Books International.

POLITICAL CULTURE, SOFT INTERVENTIONS AND NATION BUILDING

Lawler, A., 2007. Middle Asia takes center stage. *Science*, 317, 586–590.

Ludden, D., ed., 2005. *Making India Hindu: religion, community, and the politics of democracy in India*. Oxford: Oxford University Press.

Mahaprashasta, A.A., 2009. 'State should rely on historians': Interview with D.N. jha, eminent historian. *Frontline*, 26 (25). Available from: http://www.flonnet.com/fl2625/stories/20091218262501700.htm [Accessed 27 October 2012].

Mandal, D., 2003. *Ayodhya: archaeology after demolition*. Revised ed. Hyderabad: Orient Longman.

Mandal, D. and Ratnagar, S., 2007. *Ayodhya: archaeology after excavation*. New Delhi: Tulika Books.

Menon, M., 2004. VHP move foiled. *The Hindu*. Available from: http://www.hindu.com/2004/09/13/stories/2004091309450100.htm [Accessed 10 July 2009].

Misra, A., 2004. Theorising 'small' and 'micro' state behaviour using the Maldives, Bhutan and Nepal. *Contemporary South Asia*, 13 (2), 133–148.

Misra, V.N., 1992. Research on the Indus civilization: a brief review. *The eastern anthropologist*, 45.

Mitra, S.K., 2003. The reluctant hegemon: India's self-perception and the South Asian strategic environment. *Contemporary South Asia*, 12 (3), 399–417.

Mohanty, R.K. and Smith, M.L., 2008. *Excavations at Orissa: Sisupalgarh*. New Delhi: Indian Archaeological Society.

Müller, F.M., 1883. *India what can it teach us?* London: Longmans Green & Co.

Nehru, J., 1946. *The discovery of India*. New Delhi: Penguin Books India.

Paddayya, K., 1995. Theoretical perspectives in Indian archaeology. In: P.J. Ucko ed., *Theory in archaeology: a world perspective*. London: Routledge, 109–141.

Pandey, S., 2002. More fall prey to police firings in Gujarat. *The Times of India*. Available from: http://timesofindia.indiatimes.com/articleshow/8283550.cms [Accessed 4 July 2009].

Pant, H.V., 2010. India in Afghanistan: a test case for a rising power. *Contemporary South Asia*, 18 (2), 133–153.

Pappu, S., 2000. Archaeology in schools: an Indian example. *Antiquity*, 74, 485–486.

Phull, A., 2010. Chapter on MF Hussain dropped from HP curriculum. *Hindustan Times*. Available from: http://www.hindustantimes.com/StoryPage/Print/494826.aspx [Accessed 10 September 2010].

Pollock, S., 1993. Ramayana and political imagination in India. *The journal of Asian studies*, 52 (2), 261–297.

Possehl, G.L., 1996. Indus age: the writing system. New Delhi: Oxford & IBH Publishing Co.

Prakash, G., 1992. Writing post-Orientalist histories of the Third World: Indian historiography is good to think. *In*: N.B. Dirks ed., *Colonialism and culture*. Ann Arbor, MI: University of Michigan Press, 353–388.

Rao, N., 1994. Interpreting silences: symbol and history in the case of Ram Janmabhoomi/Babri Masjid. *In*: E.C. Bond and A. Gilliam, eds, *Social construction of the past: representation as power*. London: Routledge, 154–166.

Rao, P.V.N., 2006. *Ayodhya: 6 December 1992*. New Delhi: Penguin Books India.

Ratnagar, S., 2003. Afterword. *In*: D. Mandal, ed. *Ayodhya: archaeology after demolition*. Revised ed. Hyderabad: Orient Longman, 66–70.

Ratnagar, S., 2004. Archaeology at the heart of a political confrontation. *Current anthropology*, 45 (2), 298–301.

Sahu, S., 2008. Ancient city discovered in India. BBC News. Available from: http://news.bbc.co.uk/1/hi/world/south_asia/7250316.stm [Accessed 19 May 2009].

Sayeed, V., 2009. Communal work. *Frontline*. Available from: http://www.hinduonnet.com/fline/fl2621/stories/20091023262103200.htm [Accessed 14 October 2009].

Sen, A., 1993. The threats to secular India. *Social scientist*, 21 (3–4), 5–23.

Sen, A., 2005. *The argumentative Indian: writings on culture, history and identity*. London: Allen Lane.

Sharma, D.V., Hon'ble, 2010. Decision of Hon'ble Special Full Bench hearing Ayodhya matters: issues for briefing. Allahabad High Court, 30 Apr. Available from: file:/// Users/brianhole/Desktop/AllahabadHC_300910_verdict/ayodhyafiles/hondvsj-gist-vol1. pdf [Accessed 1 October 2010].

Sharma, R.S., 2001. The Ayodhya issue. *In*: R. Layton, P.G. Stone and J. Thomas, eds. *Destruction and conservation of cultural property*. London: Routledge, 127–138.

Sharma, Y.D., Srivastava, K.M., Gupta, S.P., Nautiyal, K.P., Grover, B.R., Agrawal, D.S., Mukherji, S. and Malayya, S., 1992. *Ramajanma Bhumi: Ayodhya: new archaeological discoveries*. New Delhi: Historian's Forum.

Shinde, V., Deshpande, S.S., Osada, T. and Uno, T., 2006. Basic issues in Harappan archaeology: some thoughts. *Ancient Asia*, 1, 63–72.

Singh, M.P., 2007. A borderless internal federal space? Reorganization of states in India. *India review*, 6 (4), 233–250.

Sreenivas, J., 2004. Modi government goes 'secular'. *ExpressIndia.com*, 15 October. Available from: http://www.expressindia.com/news/fullstory.php?newsid=37288 [Accessed 27 October 2012].

Srikanth, B.R., 2003. Another Ayodhya? *Outlook*. Available from: http://www.outlookindia. com/full.asp?fname=Ayodha%20(F)&fodname=20031222&sid=1 [Accessed 4 July 2009].

Srinivasaraju, S., 2009. Deccan, chronic? *Outlook*. Available from: http://www.outlookindia. com/full.asp?fodname=20090209&fname=Cover+Story&sid=1 [Accessed 4 July 2009].

Suroor, H., 2004. OUP withdraws book after violent protest. *The Times Higher Education Supplement*. Available from: http://www.timeshighereducation.co.uk/story.asp?story-Code=186193&sectioncode=26 [Accessed 10 July 2009].

Swami, P., 2002. Godhra questions. *Frontline*, 19 (6). Available from: http://www. hinduonnet.com/fline/fl1906/19060120.htm [Accessed 8 July 2009].

Tagore, R., 1917[2002]. *Nationalism*. New Delhi: Rupa & Co.

Taneja, N., 2006. The ongoing communalisation in Karnataka. *People's democracy*, 30 (46). Available from: http://pd.cpim.org/2006/1112/11122006_nalini.htm [Accessed 4 July 2009].

Thakur, R., 1993. Ayodhya and the politics of India's secularism: a double-standards discourse. *Asian survey*, 33, 645–664.

Thapar, R., 1996. The theory of Aryan race and India: history and politics. *Social scientist*, 24, 3–29.

Thapar, R., 2000. Hindutva and history: why do Hindutva idealogues keep flogging a dead horse? *Frontline*, 15–16.

Thapar, R., 2004. *Somanatha: the many voices of a history*. London: Verso.

The Hindu, 2002. Editorial: inventing history. *The Hindu*. Available from: http://www. hindu.com/2002/10/14/stories/2002101400921000.htm [Accessed 11 July 2009].

Times of India, 2009a. RSS service projects multiply ten-fold. *Times of India*. Available from: http://timesofindia.indiatimes.com/city/nagpur/RSS-service-projectsmultiply-tenfold/articleshow/5194113.cms [Accessed 17 September 20010].

Times of India, 2009b. 17 years later, Liberhan Commission submits Babri report to PM. *The Times of India*, 30 Jun. Available from: http://economictimes.indiatimes.com/ News/PoliticsNation/17-years-later-Liberhan-Commission-submits-Babri-report-to-PM/ articleshow/4721312.cms [Accessed 28 October 2012]

Times of India, 2010. Writers welcome SC judgement on Shivaji book. *Times of India*. Available from: http://timesofindia.indiatimes.com/city/mumbai/Writers-welcome-SC-judgment-on-Shivaji-book/articleshow/6149038.cms [Accessed 3 August 2010].

UNESCO, 2004. *Advisory board evaluation no. 1101: Champaner-Pavagadh (India)*. Available from: http://whc.unesco.org/archive/advisory_body_evaluation/1101.pdf [Accessed 9 July 2009].

Venkatesh, M. and Radhakrishna, G., 2003. Sink or swim with Joshi's 'civilisation'—experts at war over Gulf of Cambay claim, new samples to end controversy. *The Telegraph*. Available from: http://www.telegraphindia.com/1030203/asp/frontpage/story_1634090.asp [Accessed 18 October 2010].

Vicziany, M. and Weingold, A., 2003. Security in South Asia: outsider perspectives. *Contemporary South Asia*, 12 (2), 167–186.

Walsh, D., 2009. Hindu group to get just $175,000 in textbook bias suit. *The Sacramento Bee*. Available from: http://www.sacbee.com/news/story/1923828.html [Accessed 12 July 2009].

Westcoat, J.L. Jr., 2007. The Indo-Islamic garden: conflict, conservation, and conciliation in Gujarat, India. *In*: H. Silverman and D.F. Ruggles, eds. *Cultural heritage and human rights*. New York: Springer, 53–77.

Witzel, M. and Farmer, S., 2000. Horseplay in Harappa: the Indus valley decipherment hoax. *Frontline*, 4–14.

Wyatt, A., 2005. Building the temples of postmodern India: economic constructions of national identity. *Contemporary South Asia*, 14 (4), 465–480.

Zavos, J., 2008. Stamp it out! Disciplining the image of Hinduism in a multicultural milieu. *Contemporary South Asia*, 16 (3), 323–337.

Index

academia 90–2
Aegis Trust 35, 38, 39, 40, 41, 43
affiliation, cultural 63
Afghanistan 98
African American Lives project 57
African post-colonial states 66
Afzal Khan tomb 88
Agarwal, D.P. 93–4
Allahabad High Court verdict 89–90, 97
Ancient India (Makkan Lal) 92
anthropology 52–3, 56–7
Archaeological Survey of India (ASI) 82, 85, 89, 91–2
archaeology 52–3; and contemporary identity processes 61–8; India 81–2, 93–5; the past and identity politics 57–61; and repatriation 56–68
Arendt, H. 79
artists 9, 10
Aryan race issue 90
Ashdown, P. 23
Australia 54
Avruch, K. 17, 19
Ayodhya 83–5, 89–90

Babri Masjid Action Committee (BMAC) 84, 85
Babri Masjid mosque 83–5, 88
Bangladesh 98
Beth Shalom Holocaust Centre, Nottingham 39, 41
Bhandarkar Oriental Research Institute, Pune 93
Bharatiya Janata Party (BJP) 81, 83, 84, 87–9, 92, 99
Bhimbetka site 95
Bhutan 98
Bosnian Civil War 2, 17, 23, 25; international community involvement in reconstruction 9–10, 19–20, 21–2; memorials 18; reconstruction of cultural heritage 13–16
Brasilia 4
Brass, P.R. 81, 98
British Druids 55, 56
British Museum 55

Bush, G.W. 46

Centre for Cultural Decontamination (CZKD) 17
Champaner-Pavagadh Archaeological Park 87
civil wars 7–8; post-conflict reconstruction *see* reconstruction
colonialism 59–61; *see also* post-colonial nation-building
communal violence 86–7
community-based reconstruction projects 22
community healing, phases of 15–16
Convention on the Means of Prohibiting and Preventing the Illicit Import, Export and Transfer of Ownership of Cultural Property (1970) 55, 70
Convention for the Protection of the World Cultural and Natural Heritage (1972) 21, 22
Convention for the Safeguarding of the Intangible Cultural Heritage (2003) 1
Council of British Druids Order 55
Council of Europe 10
Croatia 16
cultural affiliation 63
cultural difference 67–8, 69–70
Cultural Heritage and the Re-Construction of Identities after Conflict project 24
cultural homogeneity 61, 83

Dayton Peace Accords 10, 16
Democratic Republic of Congo 47
demonization of the enemy other 13–14
destruction of heritage sites 83–8
diaspora culture 61
difference, cultural 67–8, 69–70
diversity 78–9
Djenné 4
Dubrovnik 9, 22
Duro, G. 12

Eaton, R.M. 86
education: genocide 38, 45; Hindutva ideology 92–3; India 92, 96–7
emancipation, repatriation as 54–7

INDEX

Eriksen, T.H. 65
essentialism 68, 69–70
expansionism 99
external agencies 4–5

fragmentation 61
France 33, 44
Franco regime 11–13

Gandhi, I. 81
Gandhi, R. 81
genocide education 38, 45
genocide memorials 2–3, 31–51; Kigali Genocide
  Memorial Centre 2, 34, 35, 37–47
genocide survivors 45
Germany 58
Gernika 10, 17, 24–5; Peace Museum 24
Godhra 86, 87
Goel, S.R. 86
Government of India Act (1935) 80
Grant, W.J. 99
Great Zimbabwe 66
Greater India Society 99
Greece 55
Greenland 55
group identities 16–17
Gujarat 86–7
Guru Dattatreya Baba Budangiri Swamy dargah
  87–8

Hague Convention (1954) 1, 10
Handler, R. 17
heritage destruction 83–8
Hindu nationalist movement (Hindutva or Sangh
  Parivar) 4, 80–99
Holocaust 32
homogenization 61, 83
Honduras 67
human remains: displayed at KMC 41;
  repatriation of see repatriation
human rights 44–5
Husain, M.F. 92, 93
Hutus 32, 33, 42

identity: India 80, 97–8; archaeology, identity
  processes and repatriation 57–68;
  reconstructing in post-war societies 16–17
imposition of a vision of heritage 22–3
India 4, 78–104; consequences of the rise of the
  Hindu right 97–9; partition 80, 82; rise of right-
  wing Hindu nationalism 4, 80–97
'India Shining' campaign 99
Indian Council of Historical Research (ICHR) 92
indigenous peoples 5, 60; repatriation and post-
  colonial nation-building 64–7; right to
  difference 67–8; see also repatriation
Indus civilization 81–2, 90–1, 92, 95

Ingabire, V. 46
intangible cultural heritage 1–2
intellectuals 9, 10; see also scholars
international community 4–5; aims of aid to
  Rwanda 35–7; failure to halt the genocide in
  Rwanda 33–4, 37, 44; involvement in post-war
  reconstruction 8–9, 14–15, 19–25, 26; KMC
  and 44–5; peacekeeping operations 8;
  reconciliation projects 47; Rwanda genocide
  memorials 2–3, 31, 32, 33–8, 47–8
International Council of Museums (ICOM) Code
  of Ethics for Museums 55
International Criminal Tribunal for the former
  Yugoslavia 22
International Office of Museums 9
Iraq 5, 66, 67
Israel 54, 56, 67

Joshi, M.M. 87
Joy, C. 4

Kagame, P. 40
kar sevaks (holy volunteers) 85, 86, 88
Karnataka 87–8
Kashmir 98
Kennewick skeleton 63
Keynes, J.M. 20
Kigali Genocide Memorial Centre (KMC) 2, 34,
  35, 37–47; created by a transnational process
  39–40; exhibition on the history of the
  genocide 42–4; genocide education and
  mourning 38; nature of the museum 40–1;
  perspective on the international community
  44–5; responses to 45–6; symbolic
  reconstruction of Rwanda 41–2
King Fahd mosque, Sarajevo 15
Kymlicka, W. 80, 94

Laine, J. 93
Lal, B.B. 83, 84, 86, 91
Law of the Historic Memory (Spain) 13
League of Nations 9
Lee, B. 14
Lemarchand, R. 43
local ideological motivations 22–3
Loir, G. 37
Lorca, F. Garcia 10; excavation of the burial site
  of 13

Maharashtra 88
Maori people 65
mass unmarked graves 13
materiality 58–9
Maynard, K. 15
Mazuka, B. 45
memorials: genocide memorials in Rwanda 2–3,
  31–51; post-war 17–18

INDEX

migration 61
MIJESPOC (Rwandan Ministry of Youth, Sports and Culture) 35
Milosevic, S. 13
minority groups 67–8; national minorities 80; *see also* repatriation
modernity 59–60
Modi, N. 87
mosques 15; built over Hindu temples in India 83–6
Mostar 14–15; bridge 10, 14, 20; Centre for Peace and Multiethnic Cooperation 25
mourning 38
Mugabe, R. 66
Müller, M. 90
multi-nation states 80
Murambi Genocide Prevention Centre 34–5
museum collections 52–3; repatriation *see* repatriation
Muslims 81
Mutsindashyaka, T. 39

Nacionales, los 9
nation-building: post-colonial 64–7, 69; Rwanda 35–6, 42–4, 46–7
National Council of Educational Research and Training (NCERT) 92
national minorities 80
nationalism: archaeology and 58–9, 60–1; right-wing Hindu nationalism in India 4, 80–97
Native Americans 69
Native Americans Graves Protection and Repatriation Act (NAGPRA) 62–3
Navaro-Yashin, Y. 18
Ndadaye, M. 42
Nebuchadnezzar 66
negative cycle of reconstruction 23, 24
Nehru, J. 80, 81, 82
Nepal 98
New Zealand 65
Ngarambe, Minister 39–40
Ntarama National Genocide Memorial 35
Nyanza Genocide Memorial 35
Nyarubuye National Genocide Memorial 35

Olsen, B. 59, 68
Opération Turquoise 33, 44
other: demonization of the enemy other 13–14; nationalism, colonialism and 60
ownership of the past 62–4

Paddayya, K. 94, 97
Pakistan 98–9
Parliamentary Standing Committee on Transport, Tourism and Culture 91–2
Parthenon Friezes (Elgin Marbles) 55
Partido Popular 13

partition of India 80, 82
past, the: archaeology and identity politics 57–61; ownership of 62–4
past–present continuity 57, 61, 62–3, 69
peace symbolism 24–5
phases of community healing 15–16
Picasso, P., *Guernica* 10, 25
plural identities 16
positivist value of heritage 20–1
Possehl, G.L. 93
post-colonial nation-building 64–7, 69
post-conflict reconstruction *see* reconstruction
Prado Museum 9

racist archaeology 59–60
Ram Janmabhumi (Birthplace of Rama) campaign 83, 89
Rashtriya Swayamsevak Sangh (RSS) (National Self-Help Association) 81, 89
recognition 64–7
reconciliation 35–6
reconstruction 2, 7–30; Bosnian Civil War 2, 9–10, 13–16, 17, 18, 19–20, 21–2, 23, 25; international involvement 8–9, 14–15, 19–25, 26; key dynamics 24, 25; memorials 17–18; reconstructing identity 16–17; re-visioning the nation 10–11; Spanish Civil War 2, 9–10, 11–13, 17, 19, 23, 24–5; symbolic reconstruction of Rwanda 41–4
regions of India 96; autonomy 98; *see also under individual regions*
religious buildings 15; temple desecration 83–6
repatriation 3–4, 5, 52–77; archaeology and contemporary identity processes 61–8; archaeology, the past and identity 57–61; global movement of emancipation 54–7; and indigenous peoples and minorities 67–8; ownership of the past 62–4; recognition and post-colonial nation-building 64–7
researchers, nationalist 93–4
re-visioning the nation 10–11; Spain 11–13
right to difference 67–8, 69–70
right-wing Hinduism 4, 80–99
rights struggles 69
Rigveda 91
Rwanda 2–3, 31–51; aid for genocide remembrance 34–7; imagining post-genocide Rwanda 46–7; international community and 2–3, 31, 32, 33–8, 47–8; Kigali Genocide Memorial Centre 2, 34, 35, 37–47; symbolic reconstruction 41–4
Rwandan Patriotic Front (RPF) 32, 33, 36, 42, 43–4

Saddam Hussein 66
Sahu, S. 96
salvage ethnography 60

INDEX

Sanskrit summer camps 92
Sarajevo 9–10, 15
Saraswati Heritage Project 91–2
scholars 90–2
secularism 78–9, 80–1
self-determination, right to 64
Sen, A. 16, 78, 97
Service for the Defence of the National Artistic
   Patrimony (PAN) 11–12
Service for Devastated Regions and Reparations
   11–12
Shao Bano case 81
Sharma Children's Museum 96–7
Singh, K. 89
Singh, M.P. 98
Sisupalgarh historic city, Orissa 95–6
Siwalik region 94
Smith, S. 43, 45
social practices of visitation 46
social rights 69
Somanatha temple, Gujarat 82
Sontag, S. 10
Spanish Civil War 2, 19, 24–5; international
   community involvement in reconstruction 9–
   10, 23; memorials 17; rebuilding the state 11–
   13
Srebrenica massacre 10
Srebrenica-Potocari Memorial and Cemetery to
   Genocide Victims 18
stateless communities 79
strategic essentialism 68
subaltern studies 96
sub-national self-promotion 65–6
symbolic reconstruction 41–4
symbolism, peace 24–5
symbols, removal of 13
syncretic history 95

Tagore, R. 78, 79
Taylor, C. 64
Te Papa Tongarewa Museum 65
technical expertise 22–3
temple desecration 83–6
Thapar, R. 93

time 23
Tito regime 13
toi moko (preserved tattooed heads) 65
Torpey, J. 5
transnational memory-making 32, 39–40
Trigger, B. 66
Tudjman, F. 13
Tutsis 32, 33, 42

United Kingdom (UK) 55; Hindutva ideology 93
United Nations (UN): peacekeeping operations 8;
   reluctance to act in Rwanda 44
United Nations Educational, Scientific and
   Cultural Organization (UNESCO) 1, 4, 10
United States (US) 12, 54; Hindutva ideology 92–
   3; NAGPRA 62–3; social rights for Native
   Americans 69
universal value 21
unmarked mass graves 13
USSR 98

Vadodara 87
Vedic culture 90–1
Versailles, Treaty of 20
victims: rehumanization of 40–1; rights to
   recognition and justice 13, 36
Visegrad Bridge 15
Vishwa Hindu Parishad (VHP) (World Council of
   Hindus) 81, 84, 85, 86, 87

war memorials 17–18
'wasted lives' exhibition 45
Williams, P. 3, 4, 41
world heritage label 21
World War II 1, 12, 13

Yugoslavia, former 13–14; *see also* Bosnian Civil
   War

Zapatero government 13
Zimbabwe 66, 67